The Mothers Legacy to her Vnborn Childe

The Mothers Legacy
to her Vnborn Childe

ELIZABETH JOSCELIN

Edited with introduction and notes
by Jean LeDrew Metcalfe

UNIVERSITY OF TORONTO PRESS
Toronto Buffalo London

© University of Toronto Press Incorporated 2000
Toronto Buffalo London
Printed in Canada

ISBN 0-8020-4694-0

Printed on acid-free paper

Canadian Cataloguing in Publication Data

Jocelin, Elizabeth, 1596–1622
  The mothers legacy to her vnborn childe

  Includes bibliographical references and index.
  ISBN 0-8020-4694-0

  1. Children – Religious life – Early works to 1800.   2. Children –
  Conduct of life – Early works to 1800.   I. Metcalfe, Jean D. LeDrew.
  II. Title.   III. Title: Mothers legacy to her unborn childe.

  BV4570.J62 2000   248.8'2   C99-931610-9

This book has been published with the help of a grant from the Humanities and Social Sciences Federation of Canada, using funds provided by
the Social Sciences and Humanities Research Council of Canada.

University of Toronto Press acknowledges the financial assistance to its
publishing program of the Canada Council for the Arts and the Ontario
Arts Council.

University of Toronto Press acknowledges the financial support for its
publishing activities of the Government of Canada through the Book
Publishing Industry Development Program (BPIDP).

Contents

Illustrations

Acknowledgments

From my first reading of *The Mothers Legacy to her Vnborn Childe*, I was captivated by the learned eloquence of its author; my first acknowledgment, then, must be to Elizabeth Joscelin, who, in her short life, wrote a book that would occupy such an important part of my life and which, I hope, will prove equally engaging to readers of this edition.

The financial support of a Social Sciences and Humanities Research Council of Canada Postdoctoral Fellowship allowed me the time and travel necessary to undertake this work. At home and abroad, numerous librarians facilitated my research. Foremost among these is David Murphy (D.B. Weldon Library), whose professionalism and patience contributed almost daily to my work. Likewise, the librarians of the British Museum Manuscript Reading Room, Cambridge University Library, and the Bodleian Library were most generous in their assistance. Several colleagues have also contributed directly to this edition through their astute advice and kind support: Christopher Brown, Viviana Comensoli, Cory Davies, Elizabeth Harvey, and Paul Werstine. I owe a particular thanks to Anne Russell, who encouraged me in this project from its inception and whose guidance was invaluable. Likewise, Cecily Devereux's friendship, wit, and scholarly example sustained me immeasurably. Kristen Pederson and Barbara Porter, at the University of Toronto Press, made the progression of my manuscript toward publication an easy one. I am also grateful for Miriam Skey's careful copy-editing and her enthusiasm for Joscelin's work.

My husband, John, as always provided a rare combination of sanity, computer expertise, moral support, and scholarly advice during times of calm and of crisis. To my daughters, Katherine and Emily, I write (as Elizabeth Joscelin did), 'read hear my loue,' for they inspire all that is best in me. And finally, I acknowledge three women whose unwritten legacies of humility, perseverance, and love have influenced me profoundly: Gertrude (Thompson) Brown, Helen (Thompson) Hughes, and, most of all, Doreen (Brown) LeDrew.

INTRODUCTION

Introduction

1 Elizabeth Joscelin's Life

In *A Room of One's Own*, Virginia Woolf laments that 'nothing is known about women before the eighteenth century' (45). Beyond the hyperbole of her assertion, Woolf gestures toward the genuine difficulties involved in reconstructing the lives of early modern women from a predominantly male-constructed historical record. In the case of Elizabeth Joscelin (1595?–1622), two sources of biographical information exist, each arising from the author's relationship with historically significant men. First, Joscelin is mentioned in biographical and ecclesiastical accounts of her maternal grandfather, the Anglican bishop William Chaderton (1540?–1608). Second, Thomas Goad (1576–1638), the editor of Joscelin's work, records details of Joscelin's family, childhood, education, and character in his 'Approbation' preceding *The Mothers Legacie, To her vnborne Childe* (1624).

The precise date of Joscelin's birth is unknown, but the year was either 1595 or 1596.[1] She was born Elizabeth Brooke, the only child of Sir Richard Brooke (1572?–1632) and Joan (Chaderton) Brooke (1574–1601?) of Cheshire. Contemporary sources maintain that her parents lived apart after her birth (Harington 84, Leycester 167). Goad, however, does not mention a separation, and he recounts that Joscelin's mother on her deathbed instructed her six-year-old daughter 'to shew all obedience and reuerence to her Father ... and to her reuerend Grandfather' (53–5).[2] Goad, nevertheless, assigns the responsibility for Joscelin's education to Chaderton, which may suggest the absence of Richard Brooke from his family. Brooke's second marriage to Katherine Nevell produced fourteen children; Joscelin's request, in the letter to her husband preceding *The Mothers Legacy*, that, in the event of her own death, her daughter might grow up with 'my mother Brooke' and 'my sisters' (52–5) seems to indicate that she remained on good terms with her father and his second family.

Perhaps because he had no male heirs, Chaderton became an influential figure in the life of his only granddaughter. A former president of Queen's College, Cambridge, Chaderton was bishop of Chester before Joscelin's birth (1579–95) and afterwards bishop of Lincoln (1595–1608). As her grandfather's sole heir, Joscelin received a generous inheritance upon his death, including two Huntingdonshire properties: Moyne's Hall, Holywell, and Boughton Manor, Southoe (Page, Proby, and Ladds 2: 176, 352). Prior to his death, the bishop provided his granddaughter with an extensive and intellectually-demanding education. Myra Reynolds, in her study of learned Englishwomen, ranks Joscelin as '[o]ne of the most notable young women of the time of James I' (29), while Goad testifies to Joscelin's proficiency in Latin (77), a language only rarely acquired by women during this period (Crawford 'Writings' 215, Warnicke 194–201). In his introduction to *The Mothers Legacy* (1852), Robert Lee compares Joscelin's erudition to that of the humanist-educated women of the Tudor period (122–3).[3] We do not, however, know the names of Joscelin's tutors (or whether she had any). In fact, nothing – apart from her studies – is known of Joscelin's life from the time of her mother's death until her marriage.

In 1616, Elizabeth Brooke married Torrell Joscelin (1590–1656) of Essex.[4] Torrell Joscelin had been educated at Jesus College, Cambridge, and Lincoln's Inn (Venn and Venn 2: 490). Childless for the first six years of her marriage, Elizabeth Joscelin continued her studies, concentrating first on morality, history, foreign languages, and poetry, and later on divinity (Goad 68–70, 81–2). During this time, she also wrote. Her poetry, which does not survive, is praised by Goad as 'ingenious, but chaste and modest like the Author' (71–2). Joscelin's only extant work, *The Mothers Legacy*, was written in 1622, inspired by the occasion of her first pregnancy and her fear of dying in childbirth.[5] Goad narrates the origin of the work:

> Accordingly when she first felt her selfe quicke with childe (as then trauelling with death it selfe) shee secretly tooke order for the buying a

new winding sheet: thus preparing and consecrating her selfe to him, who rested in *a new Sepulcher wherein was neuer man yet layd*. And about that time, vndauntedly looking death in the face, priuatly in her Closet betweene God and her, shee wrote these pious Meditations. (99–106)

Goad parallels Joscelin's passive acceptance of the dangers of childbirth (her purchasing of a shroud) and her active defiance of death (her writing of a text through which she will communicate with her child from beyond the grave). Joscelin explains her motivation for writing in her letter to her husband, 'I thought theare was som good office I might doo for my childe more then only to bring it forthe (though it should pleas god to take me)' (12–14).[6] In *The Mothers Legacy*, Joscelin expresses her belief that a mother's greatest responsibility is the spiritual education of her child. The affective basis and, at times, emotional tenor of her writing is amplified for the reader by its prophetic accuracy. On 12 October 1622, Joscelin gave birth to a daughter, Theodora, and died of a fever (presumably, puerperal) nine days later.[7] The manuscript of *The Mothers Legacy* was discovered posthumously in her writing desk.

In his recording of the 'worthies' of Cheshire, Thomas Fuller concludes his entry for Bishop Chaderton with the following biographical note on Joscelin:

His *Grand-child* a virtuous Gentlewoman of rare accomplishments, married to Mr. *Joceline* Esquire, being big with child, wrot a Book of advise, (since Printed and Intitled) the *Mothers Legacie to her unborn Infant*, of whom she died in travail. (175)

This brief remarking of her superior moral character, unusual 'accomplishments' and untimely death epitomizes the historical inscriptions of Elizabeth Joscelin's life.

Finally, a comment must be made on the spelling of Joscelin's surname. The *Dictionary of National Biography*, following the example of the first two editions of *The Mothers Legacy*, adopted the form Jocelin (10: 836); later seventeenth-century and nineteenth-century editors of the work generally favoured Joceline. The anthologies and dictionaries of women writers, resulting from the burgeoning of women's studies during the 1980s, have perpetuated these two spellings, as well as introducing a third, Jocelyn. I have elected a fourth alternative which I derive from Joscelin's only surviving signature, located in the manuscript of her work.[8] This choice is informed by my purpose in recovering Joscelin's writing for a late-twentieth-century readership: the edition is designed to distinguish the work's original form from subsequent edited versions, while recognizing the historical significance of both. It is in keeping with this intention, therefore, that I have departed from the historically predominant spellings of Joscelin's name and privileged her only autograph.

2 The Mothers Legacy to her Vnborn Childe

The Mothers Legacy belongs to the genre of advice or conduct book popular throughout the Renaissance. The mother's advice book (sometimes called the mother's legacy) represents a distinctly female subgenre appearing in seventeenth-century England. According to the conventions of this form, a mother leaves written instructions, most often of a predominantly spiritual nature, as a legacy to her children. Elaine Beilin has argued that the mother's advice book provided women with a forum for preaching, ostensibly to their children, but in fact to a much larger audience once their works appeared in print (266–7). The publication of Elizabeth Grymeston's *Miscelanea, Meditations, Memoratives* (1604), Dorothy Leigh's *The Mothers Blessing* (1616), and Joscelin's *The Mothers Legacie, To her vnborne Childe* (1624) established the mother's advice book as a recognizable literary form and influenced its later writers, including Anne Bradstreet.[9] Within the genre, however, Joscelin's advice book is unique in addressing an 'vnborn' child.

'The Letter to her husband'

Joscelin precedes the text addressed to her child with a letter headed 'To my truly louinge and / most Dearly loued husband / Taurell Iocelin.' The author's affectionate tone pervades the letter, which she closes by signing herself, 'Thine inviolable.' Writing within a culture that discouraged women from public speech and published authorship, Joscelin justifies her writing by presenting it as an expression of 'my loue to my own' (27). In her letter, she relates the emotional dilemma brought on by the possibility that she will not survive childbirth:

William Chaderton, Bishop of Chester

I knew not what to doo[,] I thought of writinge but then my own
weaknes appeared so manifestly that I was ashamed and durst not
vndertake it. but when I could finde no other means to express my
motherly zeale I encoraged my selfe. (19–23)

Later, in the opening pages of The Mothers Legacy, Joscelin articu-
lates her fear of a public readership of the work – a fear overcome by
the desire for her child's salvation: 'neyther the true knowledge of
mine own weaknes nor the fear this may com to the worlds ey and
bringe scorn vppon my graue can stay my hand from expressinge how
much I couet thy saluation' (76–9). These expressions of her incapac-
ity as an author are conventional to both male and female writers of
the period.[10] Joscelin, neverthless, legitimizes her writing by defining
its motivation as the culturally sanctioned love of a mother for her
child. She goes on to explain the secrecy surrounding the composition of her work in terms of wifely devotion. Attesting to the mutual
affection between herself and her husband, she constructs their relationship as a companionate marriage:[11]

I know thou wonderest by this time, what the caus should bee that wee
too continually vnclaspinge our harts one to another I should reserue
this to [writing.] when thou think thus, dear[,] remember how greeuos
it was to thee but to hear me say I may dy and thou willt confess this
would haue bin an vnpleasing discourse to thee and thou knowst I
<cou> neuer durst displeas thee willingly so much I loue thee[.] (102–8)

The potentially transgressive act of a woman writing is recuperated
by Joscelin's love for her husband and reluctance to displease him.
She reiterates her own propriety at the letter's conclusion: 'I send it
[The Mothers Legacy] only to the eys of a most louing housband and
a childe exceedingely beloued to whom I hope it will not be ^all
together^ vnprofitable' (126–8).

In addition to inscribing her affection for her husband and child,
Joscelin communicates in her letter practical instructions to her
husband concerning their child's upbringing. She advises him on
the choice of a nurse for the infant, the disciplining of the child, the
appropriate education and vocation of a son or daughter, and the
importance of modest dress for children. As in The Mothers Legacy
itself, Joscelin emphasizes the dangers of pride: 'Dearest[,] I am so
fearfull to bringe thee a proud[,] high minde[d] childe that though I
know thy care will need no spur yet I cannot but desire thee to dou-

ble thy watchfullnes ouer this vice' (86–9). Viewing human nature as inherently vulnerable to sin, Joscelin advocates a rigorous disciplining of the child as a means of enabling the formation of its virtuous character and ensuring its future salvation.

The importance Joscelin places on the Christian virtues of 'modesty and humility' (93) influences her attitudes toward women's education and writing. While she desires a son to be educated as a clergyman, Joscelin qualifies her desire for an educated daughter. The relative singularity of learned women in her society represents, from Joscelin's perspective, a threat to the educated woman's humility. After cautioning against the dangers of education, however, Joscelin goes on to praise learning in her sex:

> but wheare learning and wisdom meet in a vertuous disposed woman she is the fittest closet for all good^nes^[,] she is like a well ballacet[h] ship that may bear all her sayle[,] she is? indeed I should but shame my selfe if I should go about to prays her more. (61–6)

The accumulation of tropes (the closet and the ship) and the repetition of 'all' in this passage indicate the amplitude of Joscelin's praise for the woman who unites learning, wisdom, and virtue. Joscelin's choice of a nautical metaphor may be a response to Thomas Overbury's *The Wife* (1616). In his description of the ideal spouse, Overbury imposes careful limits on women's learning:

> A *passive understanding* to conceive,
> And judgement to discerne, I wish to finde:
> Beyond that, all as hazardous I leave;
>   What it findes malleable, makes fraile,
>   And doth not adde more ballast, but more saile. (41)

Countering Overbury, Joscelin employs the figure of a 'well ballacet[h] ship' to assert the stability and perfection of the educated woman. Nevertheless, the ellipsis, in Joscelin's praise, following the third 'she is,' brings to a dramatic halt her celebration of the learned woman, as she recognizes the potential compromising of her own humility. This sort of virtuous self-effacement also influences Joscelin's representation of herself as an author:

> my dear[,] thou <> knowest me so well I shall not need to tell thee I haue written honest thoughts in a disordred fashion not obseruinge

method for thou knowst how short I am of learninge and naturall endowments to take such a cours in writinge or if that stronge affection of thi[ne] haue hid my weakenes from thy sight I now professe seriously my own ignoranc and though I did not, this following treatis would betray it. (119–26)

Within the moral and spiritual framework of her writing, Joscelin's modesty functions as evidence of her profound piety and thus powerfully authorizes her words.[12]

The Mothers Legacy

The Mothers Legacy begins with an introductory section in which Joscelin explains the objective of her work. Concerned for her child's happiness, which she defines in Christian terms, Joscelin writes in order to ensure that her child will be 'an inheritor of [t]he kingdom of heauen' (18). If her child is a son, she persuades him to become 'an humble and zealous minister' (46), and if a daughter, she assures her, 'my loue and care of thee and thy saluation is as great' (55–7). Throughout the work, she distinguishes between earthly riches and spiritual well-being, defending her writing by aligning it with the latter:

it may peradventure when thou comst to som discretyon appear strange to thee to receyve theas lines from a mother that dyed when thou weart born but when thou seest men purchas land and store vp tresure for theyr ^vnborn^ babes wonder not at me that I am carefull for thy Saluatyon beeinge such an eternall portyon. (58–63)

By juxtaposing the male's concern for his child's material inheritance and the female's attention to her child's soul, Joscelin privileges the mother's influence. Furthermore, her sense of the mother's unique relationship to her child requires Joscelin's writing of the text. When she warns her child against the dangers of pride, she reasons, 'I know not whoo will say so much to thee when I am gon, thearfore I desire thou mayst bee taught theas my instructions when thou art young' (335–7). Her text is compensatory in its function, allowing her to perform the duties of motherhood after her own death. Writing her love into a text, Joscelin ensures her continual influence over her child: 'thearfore dear childe read hear my loue and if god take [m]e from thee bee obedient to theas instructions as thou oughtest to be vnto me' (79–81). In the thirteen chapters that follow, Joscelin sets out her 'instructions.'

Chapter 1 provides Joscelin's first and most important charge to her reader: 'Remember thy creator in the days of thy youth' (84). Her 'rules for orderinge thy <thoughts> ^life^' (111–12) all follow from and elucidate the biblical injunction deriving from Ecclesiastes 12.1. Writing to a child, she stresses the importance of establishing early a relationship with God 'before the world[,] the fleshe and the diuell take hould on thee' (87–8). Moreover, the pregnant Joscelin's repeated invocation of Solomon's command (84, 91, 263–4, 384–5) inevitably carries an equivocal sense; both God and Joscelin, as creators, demand the obedience of their creations, and the maternal word is authorized by its implicit analogy to God's own.

In chapters 2–10, Joscelin 'set[s] ... down one day for a pattern how I would haue thee spend all the days of thy life' (340–2). She prescribes the appropriate times for prayer, meditation, and study, including recommendations for specific prayers. She also permits 'lawfull recreatyon' (360–1) and conversation, offering 'a few instructyons ... for orderinge thy speech' (389–90). In the course of setting out an exemplary day, Joscelin digresses periodically to warn against various sins and vices: covetousness, idleness, pride, envy, wantonness, swearing, drunkenness, and lust ('a sin that I cannot name,' 563). While admonishing her child against committing these sins, she also exhorts the sinner to repent, affirming God's forgiving nature. Joscelin contrasts a gracious and merciful God – although he is also at times capable of punishment – to the malicious and scheming devil. The devout Christian's 'seruice' (485) to God and repudiation of the devil depends, Joscelin counsels, upon a continual self-scrutiny.

Having provided a daily routine for the Christian to follow, Joscelin, in chapter 11, discusses the importance of the sabbath. She laments the tendency 'theas days' (601) for many to neglect the proper observation of this day, which, she insists, forbids all labour and requires church attendance.

While chapters 1–11 address the individual's relationship with God, Joscelin turns in chapters 12 and 13 to an examination of human relationships. In chapter 12, she counsels the duty a child owes to its father and mother, drawing an analogy between idolatry against God and disobedience to parents. In chapter 13, the last chapter of *The Mothers Legacy*, Joscelin instructs her child on the duty it 'must perform to all the world in generall' (755–6). The commandment to love one another, she recognizes, is 'contrary to our wicked nature' (760–1); however, she maintains that if God is the 'author of peace and loue' (767–8), only the charitable may be his children.

The manuscript concludes at this point, and *Sine fine finis* appears at the end of the printed editions. Although the conclusion is somewhat abrupt, Goad's insistence on the 'imperfect' (124) – that is, incomplete – condition of the work requires some qualification. Joscelin has fulfilled her stated objective to provide a pattern for the Christian day, as well as discussing the distinct demands of the sabbath. She has counselled the duties of the child to both God and parents, which allows her to treat the Ten Commandments; she then turns to the New Testament and the golden rule, urging the Christian's moral responsibility to society at large. Although the text lacks the stylistic closure one might expect – a blessing of the child, for instance – the content of its argument is nonetheless self-sufficient.

3 The Reception of *The Mothers Legacy*

The Mothers Legacy was a popular work, printed seven times in the eleven years following its first appearance. The book's appeal endured through to the end of the nineteenth century, when *The Mothers Legacy* was printed for the last time in 1894. Signatures in surviving copies suggest that it was read by both female and male readers.

During the nineteenth century, *The Mothers Legacy* was most often praised for its intimate depiction of familial relations, with Joscelin's letter to her husband singled out for its moving expression of conjugal and maternal affection. Robert Lee describes the letter as 'so tender and touching ... that no human being who is not past feeling can read it without deep emotion' (124). John Grutch writes in *Notes and Queries* (8 November 1851), 'The letter to her husband, and *The Mother's Legacy*, are two of as beautiful, pious and feeling compositions, as were ever penned by woman' (4: 367). He explains his desire to have the work reissued in a letter to C.H. Crawford:

It was my intention to have printed a few copies at my own expence and risk, so much was I pleased with the tract; more especially with the dedication of the Wife to the Husband; which brought tears into Mrs. Grutch's eyes, when I first read it to her.[13]

In the same vein, an anonymous friend recommending *The Mothers Legacy* to Joscelin's American editor, Sarah Hale, writes, 'I think no one can read her letter to her husband without tears' (128). In 1920, Reynolds identifies the emotional tone of *The Mothers Legacy* as unique: 'No other work so personal and human in its appeal comes to light in this period' (30).

With the rediscovery of Joscelin by feminist scholars, initiated by the work of Christine Sizemore (1976) and Betty Travitsky (1980), interest in *The Mothers Legacy* has shifted away from its emotional expression to its documentation of ideas about women's education and authorship. In recent anthologies, N.H. Keeble includes excerpts from Joscelin's letter in her chapters entitled 'Mother and Daughter' (182–2) and 'Authorship' (267), while Kate Aughterson excerpts the letter in her chapter on education (183–4). Scholarship on *The Mothers Legacy* centres on these same issues, and two predominant trends emerge. One group of critics responds to Joscelin's writing with considerable ambivalence, emphasizing its depiction of the origin of female literary activity at the site of the mother's death. Mary Beth Rose, for instance, presents Joscelin as participating in a 'discursive strategy [of] self-cancellation followed by self-presentation' common to mothers writing in the Renaissance; such a strategy, she contends, allows women writers to 'reconcile their self-assertion [that is, their writing] with the sacrificial constructions of the oedipal plot, in which the best mother is an absent or a dead mother' (312). Rose expresses her reservations about the 'revolutionary implications' of the mother's advice book, when she concludes, 'mothers themselves disrupt the given oedipal structures simply by writing. Their valiant, if logically doomed, attempts to extinguish themselves as presences in their own first-person narratives cannot obscure the reality that they have, in fact, written books' (313). In a far more extreme reading, Teresa Feroli constructs Joscelin as a victim of suicidal depression, claiming 'the legacy she grants her child is one of despair and aggression couched in terms of maternal love' (99). Perceiving Joscelin as morbidly fascinated with her own death, these critics interpret *The Mothers Legacy* as a confirmation of early modern women's internalizing of their culture's patriarchal ideology.[14]

Offering a more affirmative reading of Joscelin, Betty Travitsky regards *The Mothers Legacy* as informed by a new theorizing of motherhood by Renaissance humanists and religious reformers. Travitsky locates in the period's intellectual climate a valorizing of the 'new mother' that renders her 'the most liberated female developed in the English Renaissance' (41).[15] Wendy Wall, concentrating on 'the rhetoric of the deathbed legacy' (289) used by Joscelin and other women writers, concludes:

> The sudden and prolific production of female-authored tracts couched in the language of will-making creates a tradition of female legacy, a form crucial not because it revealed feminine difference or marked a female consciousness, but because it provided the ground from which women publicly challenged cultural demands for their silence. (296)

Finally, Kristen Poole, in her subtle analysis of the authorial strategies employed by seventeenth-century women, argues that Joscelin subverts the conventional restrictions on women's public discourse in order to achieve an 'authorial space' from which she can write with authority: 'Through her emphatic insistence on privacy and denial of agency ... Jocelin facilitates the entrance of her text into the public sphere' (81).

The scholarship devoted to *The Mothers Legacy* is limited and significant aspects of Joscelin's writing remain, for the most part, unexamined. The importance of *The Mothers Legacy* as a devotional work, a piece of social criticism, and an eloquent example of seventeenth-century prose requires a more sustained study than this introduction can offer. Nevertheless, a brief survey of these issues will suggest the ways in which Joscelin manipulates both her subject-matter and her style to achieve an authoritative voice on matters conventionally perceived as beyond the scope of a woman's understanding and experience.

The Mothers Legacy represents a valuable example of women's participation in the Protestant literary tradition. Critics and commentators, however, have tended to focus exclusively on the problem of identifying Joscelin's faith. While Lee's introduction to the 1852 edition of *The Mothers Legacy* describes Joscelin as a member of the Church of England (125), Hale's correspondent claims the work demonstrates 'the dawn of the Puritanical spirit' (129). Likewise, current scholarship ranges from Retha Warnicke's assumption that Joscelin was an Anglican (197) to Feroli's denigration of her as a 'conventionally abstemious subject of Calvinist ideology' (92). This range of opinion supports the view that clear denominational demarcations did not exist in early-seventeenth-century England.[16] Poole alone recognizes the conflation of conformist and non-conformist thought in Joscelin's writing: '[w]hile Jocelin's text does not bear the familiar hallmarks of a puritan tract, it is most likely she was influenced by puritan theology' (87 n22). Joscelin's recommendation of prayers by the moderate Puritan Henry Smith and the influence of Dorothy Leigh's *The Mothers Blessing* (1616) upon Joscelin's own work indicate her openness to reformist theology.[17] Although her grandfather was an Anglican bishop, Joscelin may have been affected by Chaderton's own tolerance of non-conformity.[18] It is also possible that Joscelin's husband was a Puritan during the period of their marriage, since he later actively sided with Cromwell during the Civil War.[19] Furthermore, the publication history of *The Mothers Legacy* attests to Joscelin's successful negotiation of the religious tensions of her time. That Goad, an Anglican clergyman with Arminian leanings, undertook the original publication of the work confirms its acceptability to a conformist readership.[20] Moreover, the changes made in the 1684 edition, published during a time of increased religious intolerance and anti-Puritan feeling, are enlightening.[21] Joscelin's original recommendation of Smith's prayers is replaced by the more orthodox instruction, 'Use such Praiers as are publickly allowed, and chiefly those appointed by the Church' (47). Likewise, the word 'sabbath' is systematically omitted from Joscelin's discussion of Sunday observances. These emendations suggest that the non-conformist tendencies in *The Mothers Legacy* were perceived as minor ones.

More important than her specific denominational commitments, however, is Joscelin's inscription of a distinctly female Protestant perspective in *The Mothers Legacy*. Joscelin presents Christianity as a vocation ('callinge,' 532) open to men and women alike. Through her writing of a devotional text, she demonstrates the fruits of her own spiritual life, which derive from her reading and meditation. Thus, Joscelin fashions herself as a model of Christian virtue to be imitated by the reader, her child. Beyond her influence as an example, however, Joscelin's forceful instruction on spiritual matters suggests the capacity for female teaching within the Christian church. Her expounding of the Ten Commandments, in chapter 12, might evoke as its subtext Matthew 5. 19 ('whosoeuer shal obserue and teache *them* [the Ten Commandments], the same shal be called great in the kingdome of heauen']. Moreover, when she urges her son to enter the clergy, Joscelin reminds her reader 'of how great worthe the ... ^wining^ of one soule is in gods sight' (27–8). She thereby implicitly promotes the purpose of her own writing – the salvation of her child – and identifies it with a clerical vocation. Goad, in his 'Approbation,' attests to Joscelin's authority for the 'inward inriching of others' and publishes her text 'for the benefit of all those, who, by the common kindred of Christianity, may claime their portion in this Legacy' (11, 20–2). By means of publication, Joscelin's maternal responsibility for the spiritual education of her child becomes a form of public ministry.

Alongside her spiritual advice, Joscelin adopts a tone of moral authority when she draws attention to the weaknesses of her society. In chapter 9, she catalogues the most prevalent vices of her time, including conventional warnings against swearing and drinking. She advises her child not only to shun these vices, but also to avoid those who indulge in them, recognizing the powerful effect of 'custom' (520) on the individual. Joscelin's criticism of contemporary social practices is perhaps most interesting when she comments on habits of attire, a symptom, she argues, of her culture's pervasive fostering of pride. In the letter to her husband, she criticizes parents who purchase extravagant wardrobes for their children (96–9). In chapter 5 of *The Mothers Legacy*, she discusses at length the dangers of fashion: 'I desire thee for godsake shun this vanyty whether thou be son or daughter[,] if thou bee a daughter I confesse thy taske is harder' (243–5). Like Mary.Wollstonecraft more than a century later, Joscelin laments the wasting of women's time on the demands of female dress: 'oh the remembrance of misspent time; when thou shall grow in years and haue attayned no higher knowledge, then to dress thy selfe' (251–3).[22] Joscelin's disapproval of fashion fits into a broader criticism of the materialism of her society. Throughout her work, she contrasts the 'profit or pleasure' (639) of the world to that which is 'profitable to th[e] soule' (674). Finally, Joscelin expresses her sceptical attitude toward public morality at the conclusion of her work, where she contrasts the 'custom of the wor[ld]' to Christ's commandment to love one another and finds these 'iust oposit' (862–3).

Lastly, *The Mothers Legacy* represents a notable example of a woman's use of the Protestant plain style. Joscelin's writing is, at once, humble and forceful, personal and dramatic. The apparently contradictory elements of her style stem not only from the difficulty of positioning herself as a female writer, but also from the paradoxical nature of Christian discourse itself. Drawing upon a commonplace of Christian literature, Joscelin disclaims stylistic sophistication, privileging instead the sincerity of her thoughts (Auksi 19). When she praises the clerical profession, Joscelin asserts her own plainness of expression: 'if I had <eloquence> ^skill to write^ I would write all I apprehend of the happy estate of true laboringe ministers, but I may *playnly* say that of all men they are the most truly happy' (32–5, italics added). In an extended discussion of proper speech in chapter 8, Joscelin endorses a succinct and earnest speaking style, quoting Solomon's precepts against uncontrolled speech (Prov. 12.23, 13.3, 14.5.). She urges her child to 'let thy tonge and thy hart go together' (436) – advice which informs her own use of language. Writing from the heart, Joscelin cultivates a 'dialogic intimacy' with her audience, which Debora Shuger defines as characteristic of the passion or 'expressivity' of Renaissance Christian rhetoric (228). Joscelin achieves a stylistic immediacy in *The Mothers Legacy* by writing in the first person, apostrophizing her child, imitating the rhythms of spoken discourse, and anticipating the responses of her reader. At the same time, her writing is heavily laden with the imperative, as she authoritatively maps out the life and character of her child through a series of maternal directives. While Joscelin claims to 'haue written honest thoughts in a disordred fashion not obseruinge method' ('Letter' 120–1), *The Mothers Legacy* demonstrates its author's proficient understanding and use of rhetoric. Joscelin employs an extensive range of *figurae sententiae*, which the seventeenth-century preacher and author, Richard Bernard, advises 'haue an incredible power of attraction, & pull[ ] to them the affections of hearers.'[23] Although Joscelin repeatedly constructs herself and her written 'instructions' as weak ('Letter' 20, 124, *Legacy* 73, 76, 389), the self-consciousness of *The Mothers Legacy*, its sophisticated use of rhetoric, and its passionate eloquence render it a powerful example of Renaissance devotional writing.

4 The Manuscripts

Joscelin's manuscript of *The Mothers Legacy* survives in the British Library (Additional MS 27,467). A second British Library manuscript, a copy of *The Mothers Legacy* produced by Goad, is likewise attributed to Joscelin (Additional MS 4378). As a result of the inconsistent

Illustration from *Uyterste Wille van een moeder aan haar toekomende kind* (1699) (Reproduced by permission of the British Library)

spelling of Joscelin's surname, the entries for these manuscripts appear several pages apart in the *Index to Manuscripts in the British Library*, the one attributed to Eliza Joscelin (27,467) and the other to Elizabeth Jocelin (4378). The entries are not cross-listed, and to each is assigned the status of autograph.

Joscelin's manuscript is an octavo volume in modern binding; some cropping of the pages has occurred. Folio pagination has been added to the text in an unknown hand; a single page number '57,' written in Joscelin's hand, appears at the top of 32v. The manuscript consists of the letter to Joscelin's husband (1–6) followed by three blank pages, after which the untitled work begins (7–44v). Another six blank pages appear between 8v and 9. The text is divided into chapters numbered 1–13. Joscelin capitalizes the first word in each chapter and frequently the first word on a new page, sometimes adding calligraphic touches; otherwise, she employs both capitalization and punctuation sparingly by twentieth-century standards. The manuscript is written, for the most part, in a neat and even italic hand. Those variations occurring in the size and regularity of the handwriting suggest that the text was inscribed over a number of sittings. Randall Davidson, in his introduction to *The Mother's Legacy* (1894), observes in the final pages of the manuscript the 'unmistakable signs of physical difficulty or distress' (131). Although Joscelin's handwriting is somewhat less uniform at the conclusion of the text, its irregularity is not unprecedented in other parts of the manuscript, and might suggest Joscelin's haste or her fatigue at the end of a particularly long session of writing.[24] Joscelin has made relatively few emendations in her manuscript and these are generally limited to false starts, insertions of omitted characters or words, and substitutions of one word for another. The text may be a fair copy in part, since the emendations occurring in the first seven chapters tend to be copying errors. In contrast, the divisions of chapters 9, 10, and 12 all involve textual emendation suggesting they were added as afterthoughts.

Joscelin's first editor, Thomas Goad, was an Anglican clergyman educated at Eton, Cambridge, and Oxford. He held a number of ecclesiastical offices, including rector of Milton (Cambridgeshire), chaplain to Archbishop Abbot, precentor of St Paul's, and rector of Hadleigh (Suffolk). His most prominent function in the early Stuart church, however, resulted when James I chose him to replace the ailing Joseph Hall at the Synod of Dort in 1619 (Fuller, *Church History* 5: 468). Fuller memorializes him as a '*great* and *Generall* Scholar, *exact Critick, Historian, Poet,* (delighting in making verses, till the day of his *death*) *School-man,* [and] *Divine'* (*Worthies* 159). In his 'Approbation,' Goad claims to have known Elizabeth Joscelin: 'my selfe hauing heretofore bin no stranger to the Testators education and eminent vertues' (30–1). This familiarity may derive from his acquaintance with Joscelin's grandfather: Goad was ordained in Lincoln in 1600, during Chaderton's tenure as bishop. The relationship between the two families possibly dates from an earlier acquaintance between Goad's father and Joscelin's grandfather at Cambridge.[25]

Goad's manuscript consists of fifty-one folios in a binding marked 'E Biblioteca Birchiana.'[26] The manuscript begins with Goad's 'Approbation' followed by the letter to Torrell Joscelin and *The Mothers Legacy.* The hand is the same throughout and it is consistent with Goad's signature on British Library Additional MS 23,103 fol. 18. At the beginning of his copy, Goad imitates a printed book, placing the work's title across the top of a pair of facing leaves (11v/12 and 12v/13) and providing a catchword on folio 5. He uses square capitals in the title and down the left margin through much of *The Mothers Legacy.* Goad does not reproduce Joscelin's accidentals; he eliminates all punctuation and paragraphing, expands Joscelin's contractions, and imposes his own spelling (thus, altering Joscelin's signature). While he corrects the few errors that occur in Joscelin's text, he introduces his own copying errors. Occasionally letters or entire words are obscured in Goad's manuscript by the taping of inner margins and the discoloration and slight disintegration of page edges. Because of its condition and his limited skills as a copyist, Goad's manuscript is in general a less reliable text than Joscelin's own.

Neither Joscelin's holograph nor Goad's scribal copy could have served independently as an exemplar for the 1624 published edition. The printed text incorporates Goad's emendations but also corrects omissions and errors that occur in Goad's manuscript by reverting to Joscelin's original. It is possible, therefore, that Goad produced more than one copy of *The Mothers Legacy*, and that a more accurate version of the emended text was given to the printer.[27]

5 Publication History

Goad undertook the publication of *The Mothers Legacy* in 1624.[28] W.W. Greg records Goad as having 'licensed, approved, or recom-

seriously my own ignoranc
and though J did not, this
following treatis would
betray it, but J send it only
to the eys of a most louing
housband and a childe ex
ceedingely beloued to whom
J hope it will not be altogether
profitable Thus humbly de
siringe god to giue thee all
comfort m this life and hap
pines m the life to com J
leaue thee and thine to his
most gracious protectyon :

Thine inuiolable

Eliza Joscelin

Elizabeth Joscelin's hand, from British Library, Additional MS 27,467
(Reproduced by permission of the British Library)

THE
MOTHERS
LEGACIE.
to her vnborne
CHILDE

Hauing long often and earnestly
desired of god that i might beea
A Mother to one of his children
And the time now drawinge on
which j hope hee hath appointed to
giue thee vnto mee it drew me into
a consideration both wherefore j
so Earnestly desired thee and hauing
found that the true cause was toillay
Thee happy howe might compasse this
Happinesse for thee j knew jt consisted
not jn honour wealth strength of
Bodij or frends though all these are
great blessings therefore jt had beene
a weake Request to desire thee
onelij for an heire to ell

Thomas Goad's hand, from British Library, Additional MS 4378 (Reproduced by permission of the British Library) mended' 182 books between 1615 and 1631 (3, 37–8). *The Mothers Legacy* was entered in the Stationer's Register on January 12, 1623/4; the author appears as Ellen. Joslin (Arber 4: 72). The work was frequently reissued during Goad's lifetime: extant editions date from 1624, 1625, 1632, and 1635. Editions from 1684, 1722, 1724, 1840, 1852, 1853, 1871, and 1894 also survive and illustrated Dutch translations appeared in 1699 and 1784.[29] Three editions (1852, 1871, and 1894) include introductions to *The Mothers Legacy*. Since these provide evidence of the work's reception during the nineteenth century, I have reproduced the introductions by Robert Lee, Sarah Hale, and Randall Davidson in the appendix to this edition.

Goad's supplementing and emending of Joscelin's text suggests that he took on the role of an editor for her work. Fuller described Goad as 'loving to *steere* the discourse ... of all the Company he came in' (*Worthies* 159), and the assertiveness of his personality is also evident in his editorial treatment of Joscelin's text. To begin, Goad is responsible for having assigned *The Mothers Legacy* its title. His choice derives from a passage in Joscelin's letter to her husband in which she figures her work as a legacy – 'this my little legacy of wch my childe is the executer' (33–4). Joscelin, however, also refers to her text as a letter ('Letter' 31), her 'meditations' (*Legacy* 70), a mirror ('Letter' 115, 116), a treatise ('Letter' 125) and, most often, her 'instructions' (*Legacy* 73, 80, 337, 389). Naming the work as he did, Goad reinforced the identification of the mother's advice book as legacy, and thereby influenced the historical and critical reception of Joscelin's writing. For instance, later advice books were influenced by the title of *The Mothers Legacy*: Elizabeth Richardson's *A Ladies Legacie to her Daughters* (1645) and Susanna Bell's *The Legacy of a Dying Mother* (1673).

Consistent with his choice of title is Goad's emphasis, in his 'Approbation,' on the testamentary nature of Joscelin's work. This introduction to *The Mothers Legacy* is itself an important cultural document, addressing the controversial issues of women's legal status, education, and writing from a male perspective. Goad provides a biographical background of Joscelin as part of his justification for 'registering this *Will*, among the most publique Monuments, (the rather worthy, because proceeding from the weaker sex)' (26–8). While he follows Joscelin's own favouring of a spiritual inheritance over a material one, Goad nonetheless takes this opportunity to stress women's disability under the law: 'OVr lawes disable those,

that are vnder *Couert-baron*, from disposing by Will and Testament
any temporall estate' (1–2). Despite Goad's assertion to the contrary,
however, it was possible during this period for married women to
write wills.[30] In fact, Joscelin obliquely suggests that she will provide
a financial inheritance for her child: 'it had bin a poor and weake
desire to desire thee *only* for an heir [t]o my fortune' (8–10, italics
added). Goad defends Joscelin's writing and his own publishing of
The Mothers Legacy by arguing that 'vertue and grace haue power
beyond all empeachment of sex or other debility' (8–10), and he
presents the work to its original readers as a text significant to the
community of Christian believers. Nevertheless, Goad implies, by
attaching his 'Approbation' to Joscelin's work, that the spiritual
advice of a laywoman requires the approval of a male clergyman
before it appears in print.

Goad's emendation of *The Mothers Legacy* likewise demonstrates
his rather parochial attitude toward Joscelin's writing. His inten-
tional departures from her manuscript fall into three categories: corrections, stylistic changes, and modifications of content. The last of
these are the most invasive and demonstrate most clearly Goad's
own ideological commitments. Goad's interference with Joscelin's
communication of her ideas occurs in a variety of degrees. At times,
he will merely intensify or attenuate Joscelin's meaning. For
instance, when Joscelin criticizes parents for encouraging pride in
their children – 'parents read lectors of it to theyr children' ('Letter'
75–6) – Goad writes, 'Many parents ...' Similarly, Joscelin's direction
to her child to pay attention 'though thou hearest a minister preache
as thou thinkest weakly' (*Legacy* 671–2) is modified to 'though perhaps thou hearest ...' Presumably sensitive to the reputation of his
own profession, Goad also changes the devil's 'ministers' (642) to
'Instruments.' Perhaps more troubling from a feminist perspective,
Goad replaces the adjective 'learned' (283) when it is applied to
women with 'honest.'[31] Similarly, Goad alters Joscelin's concern that
her daughter attain 'higher knowledge' (252–3) than merely how to
dress herself by substituting 'other knowledge.' In Joscelin's instructions on proper speech, Goad varies the original sentence order, and
the meaning is subtly affected. Josceline instructs her daughter first
as a Christian, and then as a 'mayd' (534). By reversing this order,
Goad emphasizes the speaker's gender and implies a differential attitude toward male and female speech. Likewise, in Joscelin's compar-
ison of a male adulterer to a disobedient child, she speaks of the

former forsaking 'the wife of his bosom' (733); Goad's copy is garbled at this point, but the published version offers the more patriarchal definition of the wife as 'her, by whom he giueth being vnto others.' Finally, Goad resorts to censorship when he excises a portion of Joscelin's discussion of the sabbath (596–600). Goad seems to object here to Joscelin's 'Judaizing' of the Christian sabbath, a sensitive doctrinal issue at the time (Hill 204).

6 Editorial Procedures

The survival of both Joscelin's holograph and Goad's copy of *The Mothers Legacy* offers a rare opportunity to observe the effect of a male editor on a seventeenth-century text authored by a woman. The parallel edition that follows is designed to facilitate a page-by-page perception of the work's transmission and alteration, thus recognizing the significance of both the authorial manuscript and the later printed text. First, a diplomatic transcription of Joscelin's holograph appears on the left-hand pages. Any substantive variations in Goad's manuscript appear at the bottom of each page. The 1624 (second) impression, a social text resulting from the combined influences of editor, publisher, and printer upon the authorial manuscript, appears on the right-hand pages. The modifications to both Joscelin's text and Goad's copy resulting from the publishing process are highlighted by the parallel positioning of the texts, and a complete version of the published edition, significant for its wider and less controlled circulation than that of a manuscript, is fully available to the reader.

I have used the 1624 second impression of *The Mothers Legacy* (*STC* 14624.5) as copytext, since this edition corrects omissions found in the first impression (1624). The second impression is a duodecimo volume of 154 printed pages: Title page, sig. A2; 'The Approbation,' sigs. A3–A10v; 'The Letter to her husband,' sigs. A11–B9v; *The Mothers Legacie*, sigs. B10–G6v (numbered 1–114). Copies of this edition are held at the Bodleian Library, the Folger Shakespeare Library, and Princeton University Library. The variations between the second edition and the other surviving seventeenth-century editions are relatively few, and these are recorded in the textual notes.

I have adopted a predominantly historical approach to editing both the handwritten and the printed texts. I have retained, therefore, the original spelling, punctuation, abbreviations, and supralineal charac-

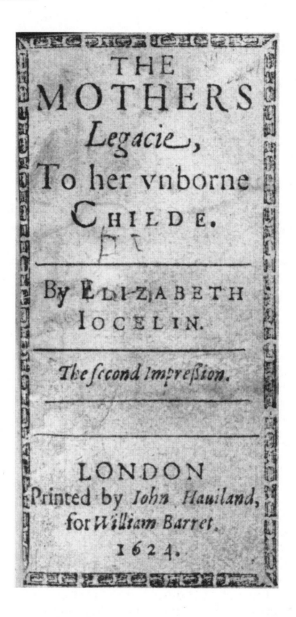

Title-page of *The Mothers Legacie, To her vnborne Childe* (1624) (Reproduced by permission of Princeton University Library)

ters in both. In the case of Joscelin's manuscript, authorial deletions
are signalled by elbow brackets < >; if the deletion is legible it is
enclosed by the brackets, otherwise the brackets remain empty.
Interlineal material is shown by carets ^ ^, and words added in the
margin are marked by braces { }. My own emendations of the manuscript appear within square brackets [ ], and these fit into the following categories:

1) changing the first letter of a new page from upper- to lower-case
2) inserting letters in place of the tilde
3) supplying parts of words which have been lost by the cropping or
   binding of the manuscript
4) supplying accidentally omitted letters and words – in the few
   cases where this is necessary, I have attempted to reproduce Joscelin's own idiom by seeking out similar constructions in her text
5) providing punctuation – since my intention is not specifically to
   modernize the text, I have often inserted commas where one
   would expect to find periods in order to maintain the run-on quality of Joscelin's writing; I have introduced unmarked quotations
   with a colon or comma.

Joscelin's use of paragraphing is sometimes ambiguous; I have deter-
mined paragraphs, therefore, by otherwise inexplicable occurrences
of capitalization or spacing which coincide with significant transi-
tions in meaning. By attempting to restrict my silent emendation to
the manuscript's format, and by marking all other interpolations
with square brackets, I intend to ensure that the content of Joscelin's
manuscript and the character of her writing will remain readily
accessible to the reader.

My transcription of *The Mothers Legacie, To her vnborne Childe*
(1624) is faithful to the original with the exception of its font, linea-
tion, and pagination. I have placed annotations at the bottom of the
pages.

Notes

1 Goad describes Joscelin as not yet having reached the age of twenty-seven during her pregnancy in 1622. I have found no documentary evidence to support her birth occurring in 1592, as maintained by Bell, Parfitt, and Shepherd (117).

2 All references to Goad's 'Approbation' are cited by the line numbers in this edition.

3 Depictions of Joscelin's learning as unusual for a seventeenth-century woman may be misleading. Margaret Ezell cogently argues, '[I]t does not appear that women's education came to a "sudden end" in 1603, or, indeed, that it declined significantly from previous generations either in quality or extent' (16).

   References to Lee's, Hale's, and Davidson's introductions to *The Mothers Legacy* are cited by the page numbers from the appendix of this edition.

4 *The Victoria History of the County of Huntingdon* mentions an earlier marriage to William Sandes (Page, Proby, and Ladds 2: 176, 352), but I have found no other evidence of Elizabeth Joscelin having been previously married.

5 Olwen Hufton estimates that 25 women in 1000 died in childbirth during the early modern period – two hundred times the modern rate (181).

6 Throughout this introduction, I quote from Joscelin's manuscript and cite her work by the line numbers in this edition.

7 Theodora Joscelin inherited her mother's Huntingdonshire estates, married Samuel Fortrey of London in either 1643 or 1647, and bore seven children. She outlived her husband, who died in 1681 (Page,

Proby, and Ladds 2: 352, 'Pedigrees' 298, *DNB* 7: 490, Wright and Lewis 9: 95).

8 It was not unusual during the period for an individual to spell her or his name inconsistently. In her letter's salutation, Joscelin writes Taurell Jocelin; her husband's signature appears on two documents dating from the early 1640s as Torrell Jocelyn (Cambridge University Library Additional MS 3400, Bodleian Library MS Tanner lxii. fol. 181).

9 Other examples of the mother's advice book include Elizabeth Clinton's *The Countesse of Lincolnes Nurserie* (1622), M.R.'s *The Mothers Counsell or, Liue within Compasse* (163[0?]), Elizabeth Richardson's *A Ladies Legacie to her Daughters* (1645), and Susanna Bell's *The Legacy of a Dying Mother* (1673). Anne Bradstreet's 'To my Dear Children' – written in the mid-1600s – is clearly influenced by earlier writers of the mother's advice book but represents a truncated version of the genre.

10 Margaret Ezell usefully historicizes women's apparent reluctance for their writing to appear in print, concluding, '[This reluctance] cannot be seen as a peculiarly female trait, but a manifestation of a much more general, and much older, attitude about writing, printing, and readership' (65).

11 While Lawrence Stone attributes the notion of the companionate marriage to Calvin and traces its dissemination in England through the English Puritan writers, he argues that it was only in early-eighteenth-century England that companionship and affection became the primary motivations for marriage (135, 325).

12 In his discussion of Christian simplicity, Peter Auksi describes the authority deriving from the Christian writer's humility: 'the state of mind that is both the cause and effect of a text or thing deemed lacking in adornment, complexity, or sensuous appeal ... is lowness or humility, and it is in Christian theology – paradoxically – powerful, exalted, and significant' (13).

13 Grutch's manuscript letter is included in British Library C. 37. c. 51.

14 Rose's remark that Joscelin 'does (obligingly?) die in childbirth' (312) suggests this internalization.

15 Somewhat more cautiously, Valerie Wayne argues, 'the subject position of a mother was a more empowering place from which women could speak and write than the subject position of a wife' (69).

16 Peter White argues that, alongside James I's pursuit of catholicity in his religious policy, '[b]oth conservative and radical protestantism were heterogeneous' (217).

17 Joscelin at times echoes *The Mothers Blessing*, an explicitly Puritan

work. For instance, Joscelin's 'I may be wonderd at for writinge in this kinde consideringe thear are so many excellent books whoos least note is worthe all my meditations' (68–70) may have been influenced by Leigh's 'BVt lest you should maruaile; my children, why I doe not, according to the vsuall custome of women, exhort you by word and admonitions ... and especially in such a time, when there bee so manie godly bookes in the world ...' (3–4).

18 Chaderton's religious tolerance is recorded by Christopher Haigh (302), Samuel Hibbert-Ware (102), Clive Holmes (92–4), and Lee (120). In contrast, the *Dictionary of National Biography* portrays Chaderton as a consistent supporter of religious conformity (3: 1341–3).

19 See Bodleian Library MS Tanner lxii. fol. 181, Page, Proby, and Ladd 2: 17, and Salzman 2: 407.

20 In a footnote, J.S. Brewer claims that Goad, upon returning from the Synod of Dort (1619), 'abandoned the high Calvinistic party and went over to the other side' (Fuller, *Church History* 5: 475n). Hugh Trevor-Roper describes Goad as a 'firm episcopalian' (64). Nicholas Tyacke, however, argues that Goad remained a Calvinist throughout his career (99–100).

21 Religious legislation enacted during the 1660s (sometimes referred to as the Clarendon Code) was intended to reestablish the Church of England following the Restoration and resulted in the persecution of non-conformists throughout Charles II's reign.

22 Wollstonecraft writes, 'By far too much of a girl's time is taken up in dress'; she goes on, like Joscelin, to reject 'ridiculous fashions' and 'singularity' in attire (4:16).

23 Joscelin makes use of all eight of the figures listed by Bernard as the most appropriate for preaching: exclamation, interrogation, compellation, obsecration, optation, prosopoeia, apostrophe, and sermocinatio (302–5).

24 The entry for Elizabeth Joscelin in *The Feminist Companion to Literature in English* claims that the manuscript ends in 'a shaky hand' (Blain, Grundy, and Clements 579); this is not the case.

25 Roger Goad (1538–1610) was provost of King's College (1570–1610) and vice-chancellor of Cambridge (1576–7) during the period of Chaderton's presidency of Queen's (1568–79). Both men were first admitted to Cambridge in the 1550s (Venn and Venn 1: 313, 2: 225).

26 Thomas Birch (1705–66) bequeathed his manuscript collection, which included Goad's copy of *The Mothers Legacy*, to the British Museum (*DNB* 2: 530–2).

27 Harold Love's conception of scribal publication (35–89) may provide a

useful understanding of the purpose of Goad's manuscript and, to a lesser extent, Joscelin's. The existence of additional copies by Goad would help to confirm the text as scribally published.

28 While claims that Joscelin's husband initiated or participated in the publication of his dead wife's manuscript seem plausible (Travitsky, *Paradise* 60 and 'Possibilities' 248, Wall 284), I have found no record of Torrell Joscelin's explicit involvement.

29 Frances Teague incorrectly identifies the 1784 edition as German (258), while Travitsky claims that *The Mothers Legacy* was 'reprinted in many languages' during the seventeenth century ('Possibilities' 248).

30 Both Mary Prior and Amy Erickson document the discrepancies between the legal theory of coverture and the practice of women's will-writing. Erickson concludes that 'coverture was – socially at least – a fiction' (226). She bases this argument on the prevalence (among the affluent classes) of marriage settlements which enabled married women to evade the law of coverture (100–1).

Prior attempts to link women's writing with their will-making; in doing so, she puts forward the example of Dame Mary Compton, whom she identifies as the granddaughter of Elizabeth Joscelin. Prior, however, has confused Mary (Fortrey) Compton – the sister of Joscelin's son-in-law – with Mary (Fortrey) Parker – Joscelin's grand-daughter ('Pedigrees' 298).

31 Sylvia Brown argues that Goad's changes to Joscelin's manuscript 'recast Jocelin's portrait of feminine virtue' (21).

Bibliography

Manuscripts

Goad, Thomas. 'The Approbation.' *The Mothers Legacie, to her vnborne Childe*. British Library, Additional MS 4378.
– Autograph, 1619. British Library, Additional MS 23,103. fol. 18.
Grutch, John Malcolm. Letter to C.H. Crawford. 1867. British Library, C 37.
Jocelyn, Torrell. Letter to Lenthall. 1643. Bodleian Library, MS Tanner lxii. fol. 181.
– Mortgage of Oakington Manor. 1641. Cambridge University Library, Additional MS 3400.
Joscelin, Elizabeth. *The Mothers Legacy to her Vnborn Childe*. British Library, Additional MS 27,467.
– *The Mothers Legacie to her vnborne Childe*. British Library, Additional MS 4378.
Joscelyn, family of. Notes of Pedigree. Bodleian Library, MS Rawlinson B76. fol. 134.

Printed Books

Arber, Edward. *A Transcript of the Registers of the Company of Stationers of London, 1554–1640*. 5 vols. London: Privately Printed, 1875–94; repr. Gloucester, Mass.: Peter Smith, 1967.
Armytage, George J., Paul Rylands, eds. *Pedigrees Made at the Visitation of Cheshire, 1613*. Harleian Society, vol. 59. London, 1909.

Aughterson, Kate, ed. *Renaissance Women: A Sourcebook.* London: Routledge, 1995.

Auksi, Peter. *Christian Plain Style: The Evolution of a Spiritual Ideal.* Montreal: McGill-Queen's University Press, 1995.

Beilin, Elaine V. *Redeeming Eve: Women Writers of the English Renaissance.* Princeton: Princeton University Press, 1987.

Bell, G.K.A. *Randall Davidson, Archbishop of Canterbury.* London: Oxford University Press, 1952.

Bell, Maureen, George Parfitt, and Simon Shepherd, eds. *A Biographical Dictionary of English Women Writers, 1580–1720.* New York: Harvester Wheatsheaf, 1990.

Bell, Susanna. *The Legacy of a Dying Mother.* London: John Hancock, 1673.

Bernard, Richard. *The Faithfvll Shepherd.* London: Thomas Pavier, 1621.

Blain, Virginia, Isobel Grundy, and Patricia Clements, eds. *The Feminist Companion to Literature in English.* New Haven: Yale University Press, 1990.

Blaydes, Sophia B. 'Anne Murray Halkett.' In Schlueter and Schlueter.

Bradstreet, Anne. 'To my Dear Children.' *The Works of Anne Bradstreet.* Ed. Jeannine Hensley. Cambridge, Mass.: Belknap Press, 1967.

Brown, Sylvia. 'Over Her Dead Body: Feminism, Post- structuralism, and the Mother's Legacy.' In *Discontinuities: New Essays on Renaissance Literature and Criticism,* ed. Viviana Comensoli and Paul Stevens. Toronto: University of Toronto Press, 1998.

Clay, John W. *The Visitation of Cambridge.* Harleian Society, vol. 41. London, 1897.

Clinton, Elizabeth. *The Countesse of Lincolnes Nurserie.* Oxford: John Lichfield and James Short, 1622.

Crawford, Patricia. 'Women's Published Writings, 1600–1700.' In *Women in English Society, 1500–1800,* ed. Mary Prior. London: Methuen, 1985.

– *Women and Religion in England 1500–1720.* London: Routledge, 1993.

Dictionary of National Biography (DNB). 22 vols. Oxford: Oxford University Press, 1949–50.

Ellis, Henry, ed. *The Visitation of the County of Huntingdon.* Camden Society, old series, vol. 43, London, 1849.

Erickson, Amy Louise. *Women and Property in Early Modern England.* London: Routledge, 1993.

Ezell, Margaret J.M. *The Patriarch's Wife: Literary Evidence and the History of the Family.* Chapel Hill: University of North Carolina Press, 1987.

Feroli, Teresa. '"*Infelix Simulacrum*": The Rewriting of Loss in Elizabeth Jocelin's *The Mothers Legacie.*' *ELH* 61(1994): 89–102.

Foster, Joseph. *Alumni Oxonienses*. Oxford: Parker [1891–2]; Kraus reprint, 1968.

Fuller, Thomas. *The History of the Worthies of England*. London: J.G.W.L. and W.G., 1662.

– *The Church History of Britain*. 6 vols. Ed. J.S. Brewer. Oxford: Oxford University Press, 1845; new ed. Farnborough-Gregg 1970.

Greg, W.W. *Licensers for the Press, &c. to 1640*. Oxford: Oxford Bibliographical Society, 1962.

G[rutch], J[ohn] M[alcolm]. 'Query.' *Notes and Queries*, n.s., 4 [8 November 1851]: 367.

Grymeston, Elizabeth. *Miscelanea, Meditations, Memoratives*. London: M. Bradford, 1604.

Haigh, Christopher. *Reformation and Resistance in Tudor Lancashire*. Cambridge: Cambridge University Press, 1975.

Harington, John. *A Briefe View of the State of the Church of England*. London: J. Kirton, 1653.

Hibbert-Ware, Samuel. *History of the Foundations in Manchester of Christ's College*. Vol. 1. Manchester: Thomas Agnew and Joseph Zanetti, 1830.

Hill, Christopher. *Society and Puritanism in Pre-Revolutionary England*. New York: Schocken Books, 1967.

Holmes, Clive. *Seventeenth-Century Lincolnshire*. Lincoln: History of Lincolnshire Committee, 1980.

Hufton, Olwen. *The Prospect Before Her: A History of Women in Western Europe*. Vol. 1. London: Fontana Press, 1995.

Index of Manuscripts in the British Library. 10 vols. Cambridge: Chadwyck-Healey, 1984–6.

James, Edward T., Janet Wilson James, and Paul S. Boyer, eds. *Notable American Women 1607–1950: A Biographical Dictionary*. Cambridge, Mass.: Belknap Press, 1971.

Joscelin, Elizabeth. *The Mothers Legacie, To her vnborne Childe*. London: Iohn Hauiland for William Barret, 1624.

– *The Mothers Legacie, To her vnborne Childe*. Second impression. London: Iohn Hauiland for William Barret, 1624.

– *The Mothers Legacie, To her vnborne Childe*. Third impression. London: Iohn Hauiland for Hanna Barret, 1625.

– *The Mothers Legacie, To her vnborne Childe*. Sixth impression. London: E.A. for Robert Allot, 1632.

– *The Mothers Legacie, to her unborne Childe*. Seventh impression. London: F.K. for Robbert Allot, 1635.

– *The Mothers Legacy to her Unborn Child.* Oxford: Jo. Wilmot, 1684.
– *The Mothers Legacie, To her vnborne Childe.* Repr. 1625. Intro. Robert Lee. Edinburgh: William Blackwood and Sons, 1852.
– *The Mothers Legacie, to her Vnborne Childe.* Intro. S.J. Hale. Philadelphia: Duffield Ashmead, 1871.
– *The Mother's Legacy to her Unborn Child.* Intro. Randall T. Davidson. London: Macmillan, 1894.
– *Uyterste Wille van een moeder aan haar toekomende kind.* Amsterdam: Jacobus van Nieuweveen, 1699.
Keeble, N.H. *The Cultural Identity of Seventeenth-Century Woman: A Reader.* London: Routledge, 1994.
Leigh, Dorothy. *The Mothers Blessing.* London: John Budge, 1616.
Leycester, Peter. *Historical Antiquities ... of Great Brettain and Ireland.* London: Robert Clevell, 1673.
Love, Harold. *Scribal Publication in Seventeenth-century England.* Oxford: Clarendon Press, 1993.
Overbury, Thomas. *The Miscellaneous Works in Prose and Verse of Sir Thomas Overbury, Knt.* Ed. Edward F. Rimbault. London: John Russell Smith, 1856.
Ovid. *Fasti.* Trans. James George Frazer. London: William Heinemann, 1989.
Page, William, Granville Proby, and S. Inskip Ladds, eds. *The Victoria History of the County of Huntingdon.* 3 vols. London: St Catherine Press, 1926, 1932, 1936; repr. Folkestone: Dawsons of Pall Mall, 1974.
'Pedigrees of Cambridgeshire Families.' *Genealogist* 3 (1886): 298.
Poole, Kristen. '"The fittest closet for all goodness": Authorial Strategies of Jacobean Mothers' Manuals.' *SEL* 35 (1995): 69–88.
Prior, Mary. 'Wives and Wills 1558–1700.' In *English Rural Society, 1500–1800: Essays in Honour of Joan Thirsk,* ed. John Chartres and David Hey. Cambridge: Cambridge University Press, 1990.
R., M. *The Mothers Counsell or, Liue within Compasse.* London: John Wright, 1630(?).
Review of *The Mother's Legacie to her unborne Childe,* by Elizabeth Joceline. *The Gentleman's Magazine and Historical Review,* May 1852, 496–8.
Reynolds, Myra. *The Learned Lady in England, 1650–1760.* Boston: Houghton Mifflin, 1920; repr. Gloucester, Mass.: Peter Smith, 1964.
Richardson, Elizabeth. *A Ladies Legacie to her Davghters.* London: Thomas Harper, 1645.

Rose, Mary Beth. 'Where Are the Mothers in Shakespeare? Options for Gender Representation in the English Renaissance.' *Shakespeare Quarterly* 42 (1991): 291–314.

Salzman, L.F., ed. *The Victoria History of the County of Cambridge and the Isle of Ely.* Vol. 2 Oxford: Oxford University Press, 1948; repr. London: Dawsons, 1967.

Schlueter, Paul, and June Schlueter, eds. *An Encyclopedia of British Women Writers.* New York: Garland, 1988.

A Short-Title Catalogue of Books Printed in England, Scotland, & Ireland ... 1475–1640. Second edition. London: Bibliographical Society, 1986.

Shuger, Debora K. *Sacred Rhetoric: The Christian Grand Style in the English Renaissance.* Princeton: Princeton University Press, 1988.

Sizemore, Christine W. 'Early Seventeenth-Century Advice Books: The Female Viewpoint.' *South Atlantic Bulletin* 41 (1976): 41–8.

Smith, Henrie. *Three Praiers, one for the Morning, another for the Euening: the third for a sick man.* London: Thomas Man, 1591.

Stone, Lawrence. *The Family, Sex and Marriage in England 1500 1800.* London: Weidenfeld and Nicolson, 1977.

Story, Robert Herbert. *Life and Remains of Robert Lee.* 2 vols. London: Hurst and Blackett, 1870.

Teague, Frances. 'Elizabeth Jocelin.' In Schlueter and Schlueter.

Travitsky, Betty. 'The New Mother of the English Renaissance: Her Writings on Motherhood.' In *The Lost Tradition: Mothers and Daughters in Literature,* ed. Cathy N. Davidson and E.M. Broner. New York: Frederick Ungar, 1980.

– 'The Possibilities of Prose.' In Wilcox.

– ed. *The Paradise of Women: Writings by Englishwomen of the Renaissance.* Westport, Conn.: Greenwood Press, 1981.

Trevor-Roper, Hugh. *Catholics, Anglicans and Puritans: Seventeenth Century Essays.* London: Secker & Warburg, 1987.

Trill, Suzanne, Kate Chedgzoy, and Melanie Osborne, eds. *Lay by Your Needles Ladies, Take the Pen: Writing Women in England, 1500–1700.* London: Arnold, 1997.

Tyacke, Nicholas. *Anti-Calvinists: The Rise of English Arminianism, c.1590–1640.* Oxford: Clarendon Press, 1987.

Venn, John, and J.A. Venn. *Alumni Cantabrigienses.* Part 1. Cambridge: Cambridge University Press, 1924.

Wall, Wendy. *The Imprint of Gender: Authorship and Publication in the English Renaissance.* Ithaca: Cornell University Press, 1993.

Warnicke, Retha M. *Women of the English Renaissance and Reformation.* Contributions in Women's Studies, 38. Westport, Conn.: Greenwood Press, 1983.

Wayne, Valerie. 'Advice for women from mothers and patriarchs.' In Wilcox.

Weinstein, Minna F. 'Reconstructing our Past: Reflections on Tudor Women.' *International Journal of Women's Studies* 1 (1978): 133–40.

White, Peter. 'The *via media* in the early Stuart Church.' In *The Early Stuart Church, 1603–1642,* ed. Kenneth Fincham. Stanford: Stanford University Press, 1993.

Wilcox, Helen, ed. *Women and Literature in Britain, 1500–1700.* Cambridge: Cambridge University Press, 1996.

Wollstonecraft, Mary. *The Works of Mary Wollstonecraft.* Ed. Janet Todd and Marilyn Butler. 7 vols. New York: New York University Press, 1989.

Woolf, Virginia. *A Room of One's Own.* London: Granada, 1979.

Wright, A.P.M., and C.P. Lewis, eds. *A History of the County of Cambridge and the Isle of Ely.* 9 vols. Oxford: Oxford University Press, 1989.

The Mothers Legacy to her Vnborn Childe

The Approbation.

OVr lawes disable those, that are vnder *Couert-baron,*[1] from
disposing by Will and Testament any temporall estate. But no
law prohibiteth any possessor of morall and spirituall riches, to
impart them vnto others, either in life by communicating, or in
5   death by bequeathing. The reason is, for that corruptible riches,
euen to those who haue capacity of alienating[2] them, bring
onely a ciuill propriety, but no morall & vertuous influence for
the wel dispensing, or bestowing them: whereas vertue and
grace haue power beyond all empeachment of sex or other debil-
10   ity, to enable and instruct the possessor to employ the same
vnquestionably for the inward inriching of others.
     This truly rich bequeather, taking that care for the prouiding
an euerlasting portion for her hoped issue, which too many parents bend wholly vpon earthly inheritance, by her death already
15   hath giuen vnto her Testament that life and strength,
whereof the Scripture speaketh, *A Testament is of force*   Heb. 9.17.
after death: Now remained the other validite & priuilege
of a Testament, that it be enacted in perpetuall and inuiolable
Record. Which in this was necessary not so much for the secu-

---

1 *Couert-baron*: according to the common law doctrine of coverture, a married
  woman (*feme covert*) had no independent legal status and was, thus, covered by
  the identity of her husband.
2 alienating: transferring (of property)

20   rity of the chiefe and immediate Legatary,[1] as for the benefit of
all those, who, by the common kindred of Christianity, may
claime their portion in this Legacy, left *in pios vsus*[2]; whereout,
whosoeuer taketh, yet leaueth no whit the lesse for others in
remainder.

25   Wherefore vpon the very first view, I willingly not onely subscribed my *Approbat* for the registering this *Will*, among the
most publique Monuments, (the rather[3] worthy, because proceeding from the weaker sex) but also, as bound to do right vnto
knowne vertue, vndertooke the care of the publication thereof,

30   my selfe hauing heretofore bin no stranger to the Testators[4]
education and eminent vertues. Whereof, I here beheld reflec-
tion cleere enough, though perhaps not so particularly euident
to those that take knowledge of them onely by this Abstract.

In her zealous affection to the holy Ministry, thereto dedicat-

35   ing, (if by sex capable) her yet scarce budding first fruits, I saw
the lineaments of her owne parentage: She being the onely off-
spring deriued from a reuerend Grandfather, Doctor *Chaderton*,
sometime Master of *Queens Colledge* in *Cambridge*, and publique *Professor* of *Diuinity* in that *Vniuersitie*, afterward Lord

40   *Bishop*, first of *Chester*, and thence of *Lincolne*: by and vnder
whom shee was from her tender yeeres carefully nurtured, as in
those accomplishments of knowledge in Languages, History,
and some Arts, so principally in studies of piety. And thus
hauing from a childe knowne the holy Scriptures, which

45   *made her wise vnto saluation through faith in*
Christ, how well she *continued in those things,*   2 Tim. 3. 15, 16.
which shee had learned, appeareth, as otherwise to those that
knew her, so here to all by the frequent and pertinent application of them in these instructions.

50   In her prosecution[5] of the duty of obedience vnto Parents I
view the deepe impression, long since, when shee was not
aboue six yeeres old, made in her minde by the last words of her

---

1 Legatary: one who receives a legacy (i.e., Joscelin's child)
2 *in pios vsus*: for pious uses
3 rather: all the more
4 Testators: the author of the will's (i.e., Joscelin's); Goad surprisingly does not use
  the feminine form, testatrix's
5 prosecution: performance

owne Mother, charging her vpon her blessing to shew all obedience and reuerence to her Father (Sir *Richard Brooke*) and to her
55   reuerend Grandfather.

In the whole course of her pen, I obserue her piety and humility: these her lines scarce shewing one sparke of the elementary
fire of her secular learning: this her candle being rather lighted
from the lampe of the Sanctuary.

60   In her commission of the office of an *Ouerseer*[1] to her husband, what eies cannot behold the flames of her true and vn-
spotted loue toward her dearest, who enioyed her about the
space of six yeeres and a halfe, being all that while both an
impartiall witnesse of her vertues, and an happy partner of
65   those blessings both transitory and spirituall, wherewith shee
was endowed.

Beside the domestique cares pertaining to a wife, the former
part of those yeeres were imployed by her in the studies of
morality and history, the better by the helpe of forraine lan-
70   guages, not without a taste and faculty in Poetry: Wherein
some essay shee hath left, ingenious, but chaste and modest
like the Author. Of all which knowledge shee was very spar-
ing in her discourses, as possessing it rather to hide, than to
boast of.

75   Among those her eminencies deseruing our memory, was her
owne most ready memory, enabling her vpon the first rehearsall
to repeat aboue forty lines in English or Latine: a gift the more
happy by her imployment of it in carrying away an entire Sermon, so that shee could (almost following the steps of the
80   words, or phrase) write it downe in her Chamber.

The latter yeeres of her life shee addicted[2] to no other
studies than Diuinity, whereof some imperfect notes remaine,
but principally this small Treatise found in her Deske vnfin-
ished, by reason either of some troubles befalling her about a
85   moneth before her end, or of preuention by mis-reckoning the
time of her going[3] with this her first (now also last) Childe:
which Treatise, intended for her childe, shee so leauing,

---

1 *Ouerseer*: an individual appointed by a testator to supervise the executor of a will
2 addicted: devoted
3 the time of her going: the gestational period of her being pregnant

recommended the same to her husband by her letter to him,
written and subscribed[1] by her owne hand, as hereafter fol-
90   loweth.

The many blessings, shee enioyed, were not without some
seasoning of afflictions, which, by the good vse shee made of
them, bred in her a constant temper of patience, and more than
womanly fortitude: especially in her latter time, when as the
95   course of her life was a perpetuall meditation of death, amount-
ing almost to a propheticall sense of her dissolution, euen then
when she had not finished the 27. yeere of her age, nor was
oppressed by any disease, or danger, other than the common lot
of child-birth, within some moneths approaching. Accordingly
100   when she first felt her selfe quicke with childe (as then trauel-
ling with death it selfe) shee secretly tooke order for the buying
a new winding sheet: thus preparing and consecrating her selfe
to him, who rested in *a new Sepulcher wherein was neuer man
yet layd.*[2] And about that time, vndauntedly looking death in
105   the face, priuatly in her Closet betweene God and her, shee
wrote these pious Meditations; whereof her selfe strangely
speaketh to her owne bowels in this manner, *It may seeme
strange to thee to receiue these lines from a mother, that died
when thou wert borne.*

110   *October* 12. 1622. In Cambridge-shire[3] shee was made a
mother of a daughter, whom shortly after, being baptized and
brought vnto her, shee blessed, and gaue God thankes that her
selfe had liued to see it a Christian: and then instantly called for
her winding sheet to bee brought forth and laied vpon her.

115   So hauing patiently borne for some nine daies a violent feuer,
& giuing a comfortable testimony of her godly resolution, she
ended her prayers, speech, and life together, rendring her soule
into the hand of her Redeemer, and leauing behinde her vnto
the world a sweet perfume of good name, and to her onely
120   childe (besides a competent inheritance) this Manuell, being a
deputed Mother for instruction, and for solace a twinne-like sis-

---

1 subscribed: signed
2 John 19.41
3 Joscelin may have been residing at Oakington, her husband's estate, at the time of
  her death.

ter, issuing from the same Parent, and seeing the light about the same time.

Which composure[1] because it commeth forth imperfect[2] from
125   the pen, doth the more expect to bee supplied and made vp[3] by practise and execution.

Sic approbauit[4]

Tho. Goad.

---

1 composure: composition
2 imperfect: unfinished
3 made vp: completed
4 *Sic approbauit*: so he approves it

To my truly louinge and most Dearly loued husband Taurell Iocelin ⚹

Myne own deare loue[,] I no sooner conceyved a hope that I
should bee made a mother by thee but wth it entered the consideration of a mothers duty and shortly after followed the apprehension of danger that might preuent me for [from] executinge
5   that care, I so exceedingly desired. I mean in religious trayninge
our childe, and in truthe deathe appearinge in this shape was
doubly terrible vnto mee[,] first in respect of the paynfullnes of
that kinde of death an[d] next the losse my littell one should
haue in wantinge mee but I thanke god theas fears wear cured
10   wth the remembrance that all things worke together for the best
to those that loue god [a]nd a certayn assurance that hee will
giue mee patience accordinge to my payn. yet still I thought
theare was som good office I might doo for my childe more then
only to bring it forthe (though it should pleas god to take me)
15   when I considered our fraylty[,] our apt inclination to sin[,] the
diuells subtlety and the worlds deceytfullnes[,] from theas how
much I desired to admonish it. but still it came into my minde
that death <would> ^might^ depriue me of time If I should
neglect the present. I knew not what to doo[,] I thought of
20   writinge but then my own weaknes appeared so manifestly that
I was ashamed and durst not vndertake it. but when I could
finde no other means to express my motherly zeale I encoraged
my selfe wth theas reasons[,] first that I wrote to a childe and
though I weare but a

---

4 for] from   5 I so] so   8 an] and   9 wantinge mee] want   16 from] against   17 I
desired] desiered I   23 theas] those

TO MY TRVLY
louing, and most dearly
loued Husband,
Tourell Iocelin.

MINE owne deare loue, I no sooner conceiued an hope, that I
should bee made a mother by thee, but with it entred the consideration of a mothers duty, and shortly after followed the
apprehension of danger that might preuent mee from executing
5   that care I so exceedingly desired, I meane in religious training
our Childe. And in truth death appearing in this shape, was
doubly terrible vnto mee. First, in respect of the painfulnesse of
that kinde of death, and next of the losse my little one should
haue in wanting me.

10   But I thanke God, these feares were cured with the remembrance that all things worke together for the best to those that
loue God, and a certaine assurance that hee will giue me
patience according to my paine.

    Yet still I thought there was some good office I might doe for
15   my Childe more than only to bring it forth (though it should
please God to take mee) when I considered our frailty, our apt
inclination to sin, the Deuils subtiltie, and the worlds deceitful-
nesse, against these how much desired I to admonish it? But
still it came into my minde that death might depriue me of
20   time if I should neglect the present. I knew not what to doe: I
thought of writing, but then mine owne weaknes appeared so
manifestly, that I was ashamed, and durst not vndertake it. But
when I could find no other means to expresse my motherly
zeale, I encouraged my selfe with these reasons.

25   First, that I wrote to a Childe, and though I were but a

25   woman yet to a childes iudgement: what I vnderstood might
serue for a foundation to better learning. agayn I considered it
was to my own not to the world and my loue to my own might
excuse my errors: and lastly but cheefly I comforted my selfe
that my intent was good and that I was well assured god was
30   the prosperer of good purposes: thus resolued I writ this ensu-
inge l^r to our little one to whom I could not finde a fitter hand
to convey it then thine own: wch mayst wth authority see the
performance of this my little legacy of wch my childe is the
executor[.] and dear loue as thou must be the ouerseer for god
35   sake when <he or she> ^it^ shall fayle in duty to god or to the
world do not let thy fondenes winke at such folly but seuearly
correct it: and that thy troble may be littel when it coms to
years I pray thee bee carefull when it is young first to provide it
a religious nurse no matter for her complexion[.] as near as may
40   be chuse a house wheare it may not learn to swear or speak
scurrilos words: I know I may be thought to scripulous in this:
but I am sure thou shalt finde it a hard matter to break a childe
of that it learns so younge: it will bee a great while ear it will
bee thought ould enough to bee beaten for euill words and by
45   that time it will be so perfect that blows will not mend it. and
when som charitable body reprooues or corrects it for theas
faults let no body pitty it wth the losse of the mother; for truly I
should vse it no better: <then> ^next^ good sweet hart keep it
not <like u> from schoole but let it learn betimes. if it bee a son
50   I doupt not but thou willt dedicate it to the L: as his minister if
he will pleas of his mercy to giue him grace and capacity for
that great work: If it bee a daughter I hope my mother Brooke if
thou desirest her will take it amonge hers and let them learn
one lesson[.] I desire her bringinge vp may bee learninge the
55   Bible as my sisters doo.[,] good huswifery, writing, and good
work[.] other learninge a woman needs not though I admire it in
those whom

---

26 to better] to a better   27 not to the world] and In priuate sort   29 god was] god
is   33 the] om.   36 do not let] let not   36 fondenes] Indulgence   38 I pray thee bee
carefull] tak the More care   38 to provide] In prouiding   39 religious] om.   39 no
matter for her complexion] make choise not so much for her complexion as for Mild
and honest disposition likewise if the Child be to Remaine long abr^a^od after
waining   44 thought] taught   45 perfect] perfect In Imperfections   47–8 for truly I
should vse it no better] om.   56 work] workes

woman, yet to a childs iudgement, what I vnderstood might
serue for a foundation to a better learning.

Againe, I considered it was to my owne, and in priuate sort,
and my loue to my owne might excuse my errours.

30   And lastly, but chiefly, I comforted my selfe, that my intent
was good, and that I was well assured God is the prosperer of
good purposes.

Thus resolued, I writ this ensuing Letter to our little one, to
whom I could not finde a fitter hand to conuey it than thine
35   owne, which maist with authority see the performance of this
my little legacy, of which my Childe is Executor.

And (deare loue) as thou must be the ouerseer,[1] for Gods sake,
when it shal faile in duty to God, or to the world, let not thy
indulgence winke at such folly, but seuerely correct it: and that
40   thy trouble may bee little when it comes to yeeres, take the more
care when it is young. First, in prouiding it a nurse: O make
choise, not so much for her complexion, as for her milde and
honest disposition: Likewise if the child be to remain long
abroad after waining,[2] as neere as may be, chuse a house where it
45   may not learne to sweare, or speak scurrilous words.

I know I may be thought too scrupulous in this: but I am sure
thou shalt finde it a hard matter to breake a childe of that it
learnes so young. It will be a great while ere it will bee thought
old enough to bee beaten for euill words, and by that time it
50   will bee so perfect in imperfections, that blowes will not mend
it. And when some charitable body reproues or corrects it for
these faults, let no body pitty it with the losse of the mother.

Next, good sweet heart, keepe it not from schoole, but let it
learne betimes: if it be a son, I doubt not but thou wilt dedicate
55   it to the Lord as his Minister, if he wil please of his mercy to
giue him grace and capacity for that great work. If it be a daughter, I hope my mother *Brook*[3] (if thou desirest her) will take it
among hers, and let them all learne one lesson.

I desire her bringing vp may bee learning the Bible, as my sis-
60   ters doe, good houswifery, writing, and good workes: other
learning a woman needs not: though I admire it in those whom

---

1 ouerseer: see 43 n1 above
2 waining: weaning
3 my mother *Brook*: this refers to Joscelin's stepmother, Katherine (Nevell) Brooke

god hathe blesst wth discretion[,] yet I desire it not much in my
own hauinge seen that somtimes women haue greater portions
60   of learninge then wisdom wch is <n>of no better vse to them
then A Maynsayle to [a] fly boat wch runs it < > vnder water, but
wheare learning and wisdom meet in a vertuous disposed
woman she is the fittest closet for all good^nes^[,] she is like a
well ballacet[h] ship that may bear all her sayle[,] she is? indeed
65   I should but shame my selfe if I should go about to prays her
more; but my deare though shee haue all this in her she will
hardly make a poor mans wife but I will leaue it to thy will[.] If
thou desirest a learned daughter I pray god giue her a wise and
religious hart that she may vse it to his glory[,] thy comfort and
70   her own Saluatyon but howsoeuer thou disposest of her edu-
catyon I pray thee labor by all means to teache her <truly
though> true humilitie though I as much desire it may bee ^as^
humble if it bee a son as a daughter[,] yet in a daughter I more
feare that vice[,] pride beeinge now rather accounted a vertue in
75   our sex worthy prays then a vice fit for reproof[.] parents read
lectors of it to theyr children[,] how necessary it is and they
haue principles that must not ^be^ disputed agaynst as[:] first
look how muche you esteem your selfe others will esteem of
you[,] agayn what you giue to others you derogate from your
80   selfe and many more of theas kinde[.] I haue heard men
accounted wise that haue mayntayned this kinde of pride vnder
the name of generous knowinge or vnderstandinge themselues
but I am sure hee that truly knows himselfe shall know so
much euill by himselfe that he shall ^haue^ small reason to
85   thinke himselfe better then another man[.]
   Dearest[,] I am so fearfull to bringe thee a proud[,] high
minde[d] childe that though I know thy care will need no spur
yet I cannot but desire thee to double thy watchfullnes ouer
this vice[,] it is such a crafty diuelishe insinuatinge sin it will
90   enter little children in the likenes of wit wth wch theyr parents
are delighted and that is sweet norishment to it. I pray thee[,]
dear hart[,] delight not to haue a bould childe[,]

---

58 desire it] desired   61 to fly] to a flye   64 ballacet] ballanced   64 she is?] she
is   67 but I will] yet i   75 fit for] fit   75 parents] Many parents   80 kinde]
kindes   83 sure] sure that   83 himselfe shall know] om.   89 diuelishe insinuatinge
sin] insinuating deuill

God hath blest with discretion, yet I desired not much in my
owne, hauing seene that sometimes women haue greater portions of learning, than wisdome, which is of no better vse to
65 them than a maine saile to a flye boat,[1] which runs it vnder
water. But where learning and wisdome meet in a vertuous disposed woman, she is the fittest closet for all goodnesse. Shee is
like a well-ballanced ship that may beare all her saile. Shee is –
Indeed, I should but shame my selfe, if I should goe about to
70 praise her more.

But, my deare, though she haue all this in her, she will hardly
make a poore mans wife: Yet I leaue it to thy will. If thou
desirest a learned daughter, I pray God giue her a wise and religious heart, that she may vse it to his glory, thy comfort, and
75 her owne saluation.

But howsoeuer thou disposest of her education, I pray thee
labour by all meanes to teach her true humility, though I much
desire it may be as humble if it bee a son as a daughter; yet in a
daughter I more feare that vice; Pride being now rather
80 accounted a vertue in our sex worthy praise, than a vice fit for
reproofe.

Many Parents reade lectures of it to their children how necessary it is, and they haue principles that must not bee disputed
against. As first, looke how much you esteeme your selfe, oth-
85 ers wil esteeme of you. Again, what you giue to others, you derogate from your selfe. And many more of these kinds. I haue
heard men accounted wise that haue maintained this kinde of
pride vnder the name of generous knowing or vnderstanding
themselves: But I am sure that hee that truly knowes himself
90 shall know so much euill by himselfe, that hee shall haue small
reason to think himselfe better than another man.

Dearest, I am so feareful to bring thee a proud high minded
child, that, though I know thy care will need no spur, yet I cannot but desire thee to double thy watchfulnesse ouer this vice,
95 it is such a crafty insinuating deuill, it will enter little children
in the likenesse of wit, with which their parents are delighted,
and that is sweet nourishment to it.

I pray thee deare heart, delight not to haue a bold childe:

---

1 a maine saile to a flye boat: the principal sail of a ship to a small boat

modesty and humility [a]re the sweetest ground works for all
vertue, let not thy seruants giue it any other title then the chris-
95   ten name till it haue discretion to vnderstand how to respect
others: and I pray thee be not profuse in the expence of clothe
for it[,] my [me] thinks it is a vayn delight in parents to bestow
that cost vppon one childe wch would serue too or three[,] if
they haue them not of theyr own[,] pauper vbiq iacet[.]
100   Thus[,] dear[,] thou seest <I> ^my^ beleefe[,] if thou canst
teache thy little one humility it must needs make thee a glad
Father: but I know thou wonderest by this time, what the caus
should bee that wee too continually vnclaspinge our harts one
to another I should reserue this to write [writing.] when thou
105   think thus, dear[,] remember how greeuos it was to thee but to
hear me say I may dy and thou willt confess this would haue
bin an vnpleasing discourse to thee and thou knowst I <cou>
neuer durst displeas thee willingly so much I loue thee: all I
now desire is that the vnexpectednes of it make it not more
110   greeuos to thee but I know thou art a christian and thearfore
will not doupt thy patience: and though I thus write< > to thee
as hartely desiringe to bee religiously prepared to dy: yet my
deare I dispayr not of life[,] nay I hope and dayly pray for it if so
god will be pleased: nor shall I think this labor lost though I doo
115   liue for I will make it my own lookinge glasse whearin to see
when I am too seuear[,] when too remiss and in my childes fault
thorough this glass discern mine own error, and I hope god wil
so giue me his grace that I shall more skillfully act then apprehend a mothers duty: my dear[,] thou< > knowest me so well I
120   shall not need to tell thee I haue written honest thoughts in a
disordred fashion not obseruinge method for thou knowst how
short I am of learninge and naturall endowments to take such a
cours in writinge or if that stronge affection of thi[ne] haue hid
my weakenes from thy sight I now professe seriously my own
125   ignoranc and though I did not, this following treatis would

---

93 for] of   94 seruants] seruant   94 then] that   97 clothe for] clothes vpon   97 my]
Mee   99 them not of theyr own] not children enow of their owne to imploy so much
cost vpo< >^n^   99 vbiq] vbique   104 another] the other   104 write] writ< >ing
111 doupt] doubt of   117 discern] to discerne   117 error] errors   118 skillfully]
skilfull

100   modesty & humilitie are the sweetest ground-works of all vertue. Let not thy seruants giue it any other title than the Chris-
ten-name, till it haue discretion to vnderstand how to respect
others.

And I pray thee be not profuse in the expence of clothes
vpon it. Mee thinkes it is a vaine delight in parents to bestow
105   that cost vpon one childe which would serue two or three.
If they haue not children enow of their owne to   There wants not poore
imploy so much cost vpon, *Pauper vbique iacet.*[1]   at euery doore.

Thus, Deare, thou seest my beleefe, if thou canst teach thy
little one humility, it must needs make thee a glad father.
110   But I know thou wonderest by this time what the cause
should bee that we two continually vnclasping our hearts one
to the other, I should reserue this to writing. Whe[n] thou
thinkest thus, deare, remember how grieuous it was to thee but
to heare mee say, I may die, and thou wilt confesse this would
115   haue beene an vnpleasant discourse to thee, and thou knowest I
neuer durst displease thee willingly, so much I loue thee. All I
now desire is, that the vnexpectednesse of it make it not more
grieuous to thee. But I know thou art a Christian, and therefore
will not doubt of thy patience.
120   And though I thus write to thee, as heartily desiring to be
religiously prepared to die, yet, my deare, I despaire not of life,
nay, I hope and daily pray for it, if so God will be pleased.

Nor shall I thinke this labour lost, though I doe liue: for I will
make it my owne looking-glasse, wherein to see when I am too
125   seuere, when too remisse, and in my childes fault through this
glasse to discerne mine owne errors. And I hope God will so
giue me his grace, that I shall more skilfully act than apprehend
a mothers duty.

My deare, thou knowest me so well, I shall not need to tell
130   thee, I haue written honest thoughts in a disordered fashion,
not obseruing method. For thou knowest how short I am of
learning and naturall endowments to take such a course in
writing. Or if that strong affection of thine haue hid my weaknesse from thy sight, I now professe seriously my owne igno-
135   rance: and though I did not, this following Treatise would

---

1 *Pauper vbique iacet*: 'a poor man everywhere lies low,' Ovid's *Fasti* 1. 218

betray it, but I send it only to the eys of a most louing housband and a childe exceedingely beloued to whom I hope it will not be ^all together^ vnprofitable[.]

Thus humbly desiringe god to giue thee all comfort in this
130   life and happines in the life to com I leaue thee and thine to his most gracious protectyon:

Thine inviolable

Eliza Ioscelin

---

126 betray] bewray   127 and] and of   133 Ioscelin] Iocelin

bewray[1] it: But I send it onely to the eies of a most louing Husband, and of a childe exceedingly beloued, to whom I hope it will not be altogether vnprofitable.

    Thus humbly desiring God to giue thee all comfort in this
140   life, and happinesse in the life to come, I leaue thee and thine to his most gracious protection.

Thine inuiolable,

Eliza. Iocelin.

---

1 bewray: reveal

[The Mothers Legacy to her Vnborn Childe]

Hauinge longe[,] often and earnestly desired of god that I might
be a mother to one of his children, and the time now drawinge
on wch I hope he hathe appoynted to giue thee vnto me, it drew
me into a consideratyon bothe whearfore I so earnestly desired
5   thee and (hauinge found that the true cause; was to make thee
happy) how I might compas this happines for thee, I knew it
consisted not in honor[,] wealthe[,] strengthe of body or frends
(though all theas are great blessings), thearfore it had bin a poor
and weake desire to desire thee only for an heir [t]o my for-
10   tune[,] no I neuer aymed at so poore an inheritance for thee as
the whole world: neyther would I haue begged <thee> of god so
much payn as I know I must endure to haue only possest thee
wth earthly riches of wch to day thou maiest be a great ma[n,] to
morrow A poore beggar: nor did a hope to dandle thy infancy
15   moue me to desire thee for I know all the delight a parent can
take in a childe is Hony mingled wth gall[.] but the true reason
that I haue so often kneeled to god for thee is that thou mightest bee an inheritor of [t]he kingdom of heauen to wch end I
humbly beseech allmighty god thou mayst bend all thy actions
20   and if it be his blessed will giue thee so plentifull a mesure of
his grace that thou mayst serue him as his minister, if he make
thee a man:

THE / MOTHERS / LEGACIE / to her vnborne / CHILDE   **8–9** poor and weake
desire] weake Request

THE *MOTHERS* LEGACIE, *To her vnborne* Childe.

HAuing long, often and earnestly desired of God, that I might
bee a mother to one of his children, and the time now drawing
on, which I hope hee hath appointed to giue thee vnto mee: It
drew mee into a consideration both wherefore I so earnestly
desired thee, and (hauing found that the true cause was to make
thee happy) how I might compasse[1] this happinesse for thee.

I knew it consisted not in honour, wealth, strength of body or
friends (though all these are great blessings) therefore it had
beene a weake request to desire thee onely for an heire to my
fortune. No, I neuer aimed at so poore an inheritance for thee,
as the whole world: Neither would I haue begged of God so
much paine, as I know I must endure, to haue only possest thee
with earthly riches, of which to day thou maist bee a great man,
to morrow a poore begger. Nor did an hope to dandle[2] thy
infancy moue mee to desire thee. For I know all the delight a
Parent can take in a childe is hony mingled with gall.

But the true reason that I haue so often kneeled to God for
thee, is, that thou mightest bee an inheritour of the Kingdome
of Heauen. To which end I humbly beseech Almightie God thou
maiest bend all thy actions, and (if it bee his blessed will) giue
thee so plentifull a measure of his grace, that thou maiest serue
him as his Minister, if he make thee a man.

---

1 compasse: attain
2 dandle: play with, or bounce, a child on one's knee

it is true that this age houlds it a most contemptible office fit
only for poor mens children[,] younger brothers and such as
25   haue no other means to liue, but for gods sake be not discoraged
wth theas vayn speeches but fortefy your selfe wth remembringe
of how great worthe the <saluation> ^wining^ of one soule is in
gods sight [a]nd you shall quickly finde how great a place it is to
be a priest vnto the liuinge god[.] if it will pleas him to moue
30   your hart wth his holy Spirit it will glow and burn wth zeale to
doo him seruice, Oh L open thy lips that thy mouthe may shew
forthe his prays. if I had <eloquence> ^skill to write^ I would
write all I apprehend of the happy estate of true laboringe ministers, but I may playnly say that of all men they are the most
35   truly happy[,] they are familiar wth god[,] they labor in his vine-
yard wth out ceasing and they are so beloued of him that he
giues them abundance of knowledge[.] Oh be one of them[,] let
not the scorn of euill men hinder thee[,] look how god hathe
provided for thee sufficient means[,] thou needest not hinder
40   thy study to look out for liuinge as the Iseralites hindered theyr
work to look for straw, if thou beest not content wth this thou
willt not bee wth more. god deliuer thee from couetousnes. I
desire thee that though thou takest a spirituall callinge thou
willt not seek after the liuings of the church nor promotions
45   [t]hough I honor them as I haue great cause. but I would haue
thee so truly an humble and zealous minister that thy only end
should be to doo god seruice wth out desire of any thing to thy
selfe saue the kingedom of heauen. yet as I would not haue thee
seek theas things so I would haue thee as carefull not to neglect
50   gods blessings, but wth all thankefullnes to receyve what he
bestowes, and to be a carefull steward distributinge it to all that
haue need. I could not choose but manifest this desire in
writinge least it should pleas god to depriue me of time to
speake and if thou beest a daughter thou mayst pe^r^haps
55   thinke I haue lost my labor but read on and thou shalt see my
loue

---

31 Oh] the   34 they] they by their calling   36 wth out ceasing] om.
44 nor] not   51 all] those

It is true that this age holds it a most contemptible office, fit
only for poore mens children, younger brothers, and such as
25   haue no other meanes to liue. But for Gods sake bee not discouraged with these vaine speeches; but fortifie your selfe with
remembring of how great worth the winning of one soule is in
Gods sight, and you shall quickly finde how great a place it is to
be a Priest vnto the liuing God. If it will please him to moue
30   your heart with his holy Spirit, it will glow and burne with
zeale to doe him seruice. The Lord open thy lips, that thy
mouth may shew forth his praise.[1]

If I had skill to write, I would write all I apprehend of the
happy estate of true labouring Ministers: but I may plainly
35   say that of all men they by their calling are the most truly
happy; they are familiar with God, they labour in his Vine-
yard, and they are so beloued of him, that hee giues them
abundance of knowledge. Oh bee one of them, let not the
scorne of euill men hinder thee. Look how GOD hath pro-
40   uided for thee sufficient meanes; thou needest not hinder thy
study to looke out for liuing, as the Israelites hindred their
worke to looke for straw[2]: If thou beest not content with
this, thou wilt not bee with more; GOD deliuer thee from
couetousnesse.
45   I desire thee that though thou takest a spirituall calling, thou
wilt not seeke after the liuings of the Church,[3] nor promotions,
though I honour them as I haue great cause, but I would haue
thee so truly an humble and zealous Minister, that thy onely
end should bee to doe God seruice, without desire of any thing
50   to thy selfe, saue the Kingdome of Heauen. Yet as I would not
haue thee seeke these things, so I would haue thee as carefull
not to neglect Gods blessings, but with all thankfulnesse to
receiue what hee bestowes, and to bee a carefull steward, dis-
tributing it to those that haue need.
55   I could not chuse but manifest this desire in writing, lest it
should please God to depriue mee of time to speake.

And if thou beest a daughter, thou maist perhaps thinke I
haue lost my labour; but reade on, and thou shalt see my loue

---

1 Psalm 51. 15
2 Exodus 5. 6–23
3 liuings of the Church: benefices

and care of thee and thy saluation is as great as if thou weart a
son and my fear greater: it may peradventure when thou comst
to som discretyon appear strange to thee to receyve theas lines
60   from a mother that dyed when thou weart born but when thou
seest men purchas land and store vp tresure for theyr ^vnborn^
babes wonder not at me that I am carefull for thy Saluatyon beeinge such an eternall portyon. and not knowinge whether I shall
liue to instruct thee when thou art born let me not be blamed
65   thoughe I write to thee before. whoo would not condem me if I
should be careless of thy body while it is wth in me: sure a far
greater care belongs to the soule[,] to bothe theas cares I will
endeuor my selfe so longe as I liue, agayn I may be wonderd at
for writing in this kinde consideringe thear are so many excel-
70   lent books whoos least note is worthe all my meditations: I
confess it [a]nd thus excuse my selfe[,] first I write not to the
world but to mine own childe. whoo it may bee will more profit
by a few weak instructions cominge from a dead mother (whoo
cannot euery day prays or reprooue it as it deserues) then far
75   better from much more learned[.] theas things considered
neyther the true knowledge of mine own weaknes nor the fear
this may com to the worlds ey and bringe scorn vppon my graue
can stay my hand from expressinge how much I couet thy saluation[.] thearfore dear childe read hear my loue and if god take
80   [m]e from thee bee obedient to theas instructions as thou
oughtest to be vnto me[.] I haue learnt them out of gods word[,]
I beseech him that they may bee profitable to thee[.]

1

The first charge I giue thee I learned of Salomon Eccl: 12 1.
Remember thy creator in the days of thy youth. it is an excel-
85   lent beginninge and a fit lesson for a childe[.] looke w^th {what}
the vessell is first seasoned[,] it retayns the taste and if thou
beginnest to remember to serue god when thou art young before
the world[,] the fleshe and the diuell take hould on thee god will
loue thee and send [h]is holy spirit to take possession of thee
90   whoo shall resist those enemis and not suffer them to hurt thee.

---

67 the] thy   68 may] may perhaps   71 first] *om.*   74 then] than by

60 and care of thee and thy saluation is as great, as if thou wert a
sonne, and my feare greater.

It may peraduenture when thou comest to some discretion,
appeare strange to thee to receiue these lines from a Mother
that died when thou wert borne, but when thou seest men purchase land, and store vp treasure for their vnborne babes, won-
65 der not at mee that I am carefull for thy saluation, being such
an eternall portion: and not knowing whether I shall liue to
instruct thee when thou art borne, let mee not bee blamed
though I write to thee before. Who would not condemne mee if
I should bee carelesse of thy body while it is within me? Sure a
70 farre greater care belongs to thy soule, to both these cares I will
endeuour my selfe so long as I liue.

Againe, I may perhaps bee wondred at for writing in this
kinde, considering there are so many excellent bookes, whose
least note is worth all my meditations. I confesse it, and thus
75 excuse my selfe. I write not to the world, but to mine own
childe, who it may be, will more profit by a few weake instructions comming from a dead mother (who cannot euery day
praise or reproue it as it deserues) than by farre better from
much more learned. These things considered, neither the true
80 knowledge of mine owne weaknesse, nor the feare this may
come to the worlds eie, and bring scorne vpon my graue, can
stay my hand from expressing how much I couet thy saluation.

Therefore, deare childe, reade here my loue, and if God take
mee from thee, bee obedient to these instructions, as thou
85 oughtest to bee vnto mee, I haue learnt them out of Gods Word,
I beseech him that they may be profitable to thee.

1

The first charge I giue thee, I learned of *Solomon, Eccles.*
12. 1. Remember thy Creator in the dayes of thy youth. It is an
excellent beginning, and a fit lesson for a childe. Looke with
90 what the Vessell is first seasoned, it retaines the taste: and if
thou beginnest to remember to serue GOD when thou art
young, before the world, the flesh, and the deuill take hold on
thee, God will loue thee, and send his holy Spirit to take possession of thee, who shall resist those enemies, and not suffer
95 them to hurt thee.

to moue thy hart to remember thy creator betimes, meditate
vppon the benefits thou continually receyvest: first how he
hathe created thee when thou weart nothinge. redeemed thee
by the deathe of his only son, when thou weart wors then noth-
95   inge. and how of mear grace he hathe giuen thee his holy spirit,
sanctifying thee to an eternall kingedom. thou canst not possibly vnderstand how great theas mercys are, but strayght thy
soule must cry[:] what shall I doo for so gracious a god[?] [a]ll the
powrs of my soule and body will I giue to his seruice[.] My first
100   thoughts will I dedicate to him. like Abells sacrifice I will
present to him the first frutes of my youthe[,] in the strengthe of
my age I will fall down before him and if I liue to ould age that
weaknes will not let my knees bow nor my hands be lifted vp
yet shall my hart meditate on his goodnes night and day, and
105   my tong shall bee allways tellinge of his marveylous works.
when thou hast thus remembred the infinit mercys of god it
behooues the to settle thy selfe to a constant seruice of him[,]
[t]o order thy thoughts[,] words and actions to his glory and to
couenant wth thy selfe that thou wilt not breake thy promises
110   to god. that thou maiest the more esily perform theas dutis
Marke I pray thee theas followinge rules for orderinge thy
<thoughts> ^life^[.] spend the day as I instruct thee and god will
blesse thee and all thy good endeuors[.]

2

At thy first wakinge in the morninge be carefull of thy selfe
115   that thou harbor in thy brayn no vayn or vnprofitable but of all
no vngodly fancy to hinder thy morning sacrifice but strayght
frame thy selfe to meditate on the mercis of god[,] [t]he mali-
ciousnes of the diuell and thine own weaknes, thine own
weaknes is apparant to thee for euen but now thine eys wear
120   closed[,] thou couldst not see to defend thy selfe[,] thy strengthe
was gon so that thou weart not able to resist the weakest creature[,] a <f>gnat or a flea might glut themselues wth thy bloud:
The diuells malice is as easily perceyved for euen now he lyes
lurkinge ready to catch euery good motion from th<ee>y hart[,]

___

94–5 by the deathe ... then nothinge] being worse than nought   95 how] now
99 My first] and My   102 I will] will I   109 not breake thy promises] om.
111–13 thy <thoughts> ... will blesse] om.   118–19 thine own weaknes] om.

To moue thy heart to remember thy Creator betimes, meditate vpon the benefits thou continually receiuest: First, how
hee hath created thee when thou wert nothing, redeemed thee
being worse than nought, and now of meere grace he hath giuen
100 thee his holy Spirit, sanctifying thee to an eternall Kingdome.
Thou canst not possibly vnderstand how great these mercies
are, but straight thy soule must cry, What shall I doe for so gracious a God? All the powers of my soule and bodie will I giue to
his seruice, my first thoughts will I dedicate to him, like *Abels*
105 sacrifice[1] I will present to him the first fruits of my youth; In
the strength of my age will I fall downe before him, and if I liue
to old age, that weaknesse will not let my knees bow, nor my
hands bee lifted vp, yet shall my heart meditate on his goodnesse night and day, and my tongue shall be alwaies telling of
110 his maruellous works.

When thou hast thus remembred the infinite mercies of God,
it behoues thee to settle thy selfe to a constant seruice of him,
to order thy thoughts, words and actions to his glory, and to
couenant with thy selfe that thou wilt not breake thy promises
115 to God. That thou maist the more easily performe these duties,
marke I pray thee these following rules for ordering thy life, and
God will blesse thee and all thy good endeuours.

2

At thy first waking in the morning, be carefull of thy selfe,
that thou harbor in thy braine no vaine or vnprofitable, but of
120 all no vngodly fancy to hinder thy morning sacrifice[2], but
straight frame thy selfe to meditate on the mercies of God, the
maliciousnesse of the deuill, and thine owne weaknesse.

Thine owne weaknesse is apparant to thee: for euen but now
thine eyes were closed, thou couldst not see to defend thy selfe,
125 thy strength was gone, so that thou wert not able to resist the
weakest creature, a gnat or a flea might glut themselues with
thy bloud.

The Deuils malice is as easily perceiued, for euen now hee
lies lurking ready to catch euery good motion from thy heart,

---

1 Genesis 4.4
2 sacrifice: prayer of thanksgiving

125 suggestin[g] things more delightfull to thy fancy and per-
     swadinge thee to defer thy seruice of god though but for a little
     while but be warned and armed [a]gaynst his tentations for bee
     assured if thou once yeeld to neglect prayinge to god but one
     halfe houre when that time coms thou shallt finde thy selfe far
130 more vnapt[,] thy hart more dull to pray then before: wheare as
     if thou disposest thy selfe to pray though thou beest heauie and
     vncheerfull in it yet god whoo searches the hart and sees thy
     desire to pray though thou canst not will enlighten thee and
     prepare thy hart agaynst the next time that thou shalt finde
135 comfort. thearefore take heed the diuell deceyue you not for
     you see his malice is not small that seeks to cosen you of all
     happines present and to com for bee [a]ssured you can take noe
     true Ioy in earthly plesures no longer then you seek after
     heauen.
140   Hauinge thus discernd The infinit malice of the diuell and
     your own exceedinge weaknes how do you thinke you wear pre-
     serued from his snares while you slept or do you thinke he only
     besets you when you are awake? no be not deceyved[,] he is not
     so fayr an enemy[,] his hate is such to you that if hee could hee
145 would tear your body and drag your soule too hell while you
     sle^e^p<t>e. Alas all this hee might haue don your strength was
     small to resist him[,] now [y]ou must needs confess whoo it is
     that is only able to preserue you[,] that it is god and that it is his
     mercy not your desert that you are preserued, and gather to
150 your selfe a strong resolution wth all your force to serue him all
     the day and to resist all the tentatyons of the diuell: Then bee-
     inge thoroughly awake (for sure god likes not sleepy prayr)
     begin to giue <hi> God thanks and to desire the continuance of
     his mercy towards thee in theas words till thou canst finde such
155 as may better expresse thine own soule[:]
          Oh Eternall God gracious from the begininge and mercifull to
     the later endinge o<I>f <gi>thee world, I giue thee humble
     thanks that accordinge to thine abundant goodnes thou hast
     graciously defended me this night from all dangers that might

---

130 suggesting things more delightfull to thy fancy, and perswading
thee to deferre thy seruice of God though but for a little while.
But bee warned and armed against his tentations[1]; for bee
assured if thou once yeeld to neglect praying to God, but one
halfe houre, when that time comes thou shalt finde thy selfe
135 farre more vnapt, and thy heart more dull to pray than before:
whereas if thou disposest thy selfe to pray, though thou beest
heauy and vncheerefull in it, yet God, who searches the heart,
and sees thy desire to pray, though thou canst not, will en-
lighten thee and prepare thy heart against the next time, that
140 thou shalt finde comfort. Therefore, take heed the Deuill deceiue you not, for you see his malice is not small that seekes
to cousen you of[2] all happinesse present and to come: For bee
assured you can take no true ioy in earthly pleasures, no longer
than you seeke after heauenly.
145 Hauing thus discerned the infinite malice of the Deuill, and
your owne exceeding weaknesse, how doe you thinke you were
preserued from his snares while you slept? or doe you thinke
hee onely besets you when you are awake? No, bee not de-
ceiued, hee is not so faire an enemy: his hate is such to you,
150 that if hee could hee would teare your body and drag your soule
to hell while you slept. Alas, all this hee might haue done, your
strength was small to resist him. Now you must needs confesse
who it is that is only able to preserue you, that it is God, and
that it is his mercy, not your desert, that you are preserued: and
155 gather to your selfe a strong resolution with all your force to
serue him all the day, and to resist all the tentations of the
deuill.
Then being thorowly awake (for sure God likes not sleeping
prayer) begin to giue God thankes, and to desire the continu-
160 ance of his mercy towards thee in these words, till thou canst
finde such as may better expresse thine owne soule.
'O eternall God, gracious from the beginning, and mercifull
to the latter ending of the world, I giue thee humble thankes,
that according to thine abundant goodnesse, thou hast gra-
165 ciously defended mee this night from all dangers that might

---

1 tentations: temptations
2 cousen you of: cheat you out of

160   haue happened vnto me, I beseech thee continue this thy favor-
able goodnes toward me and so grant mee thy grace that in all
my thoughts[,] words and actions I may seek thy glory and <so>
euermore so liue in thy fear that I may dy in thy fauor for thy
son my only sauiors sake[,] amen[.]

3

165   Hauinge thus invited god into your soule take heed you offend
not agaynst so great and glorious a guest, thinke if thou seest a
superior entertayned wth such obseruance of the m^r[,] such diligence in the seruants[,] such a generall care that all things may
giue a testimony of his wellcom, Oh think[,] sinfull soule[,]
170   what care oughtest thou to haue when the liuinge god vouchsafes to dwell in thee, Oh watch[,] oh be wary: do not[,] my
deare childe[,] oh do not willfully offend him for hardly are presumptuous sins forgiuen but if out of weakenes thou offend
agaynst him run strayght before hee can bee gon for he is merci-
175   full and will stay a while after thou hast sinned to expect thy
repentance but if thou doest not make hast then the diuell
whoo will not delay to seek thy [d]estruction hee will accuse
thee mockinge thy impiety and god will leaue thee more
offended at thy neglect or rather contempt of his mercy then at
180   thy first offence[.] thearfore run quickly[,] esteem no sin small
but what member soeuer caused the to offend him bringe it
before him and let it assist thee cheefly in thy repentance[.] if
thine ey teache thee wantonnes, couetousnes or the like let
them powr forthe tears to purchase thee a pardon[,] if thy tonge
185   haue offended toward god ^or^ thy neyghbor bringe it wth
shame and sorrow to confess in priuat what it was not ashamed
to glory of in publik[.] learn to be ashamed to comit sin but beeinge comitted hope not to hide it from god by any other means
then harty repentance[,] so indeed thou [m]ayst win his mercy
190   to couer thy transgression and in his sons passion he will berry
thine offences so as he will hide them from himselfe[.] but then
thou must delay no time[,] go quickly[,] get thee alone[,] go wear
thy knees[,] wring thy hands[,] beat thy brest[,] know as little
measure in thy sorrow as thou didst in thy sin. the lord will not
195   dispise a contrite hart and though he let thee

172 do] *om.*   178 thee more] thee being more   189 then] than by   192 go wear]
weare

haue happened vnto mee. I beseech thee continue this thy fa-
uourable goodnesse toward mee, and so grant mee thy grace,
that in all my thoughts, words, and actions I may seeke thy
glory, and euermore so liue in thy feare, that I may die in thy
170 fauour, for thy Sonne my onely Sauiours sake. *Amen.* [']

3

Hauing thus inuited God into your soule, take heed you
offend not against so great and glorious a guest: Thinke if thou
seest a superior entertained with such obseruance of the Master, such diligence in the seruants, such a generall care that all
175 things may giue a testimony of his welcome, O thinke, sinfull
soule, what care oughtest thou to haue when the liuing God
vouchsafes to dwell in thee: Oh watch, Oh be wary. Doe not
(my deare Childe) Oh, not wilfully offend him, for hardly are
presumptuous sinnes forgiuen: but if out of weaknesse thou
180 offend against him, runne straight before hee can bee gone, for
hee is mercifull, and will stay a while after thou hast sinned to
expect thy repentance: but if thou doest not make haste, then
the deuill, who will not delay to seeke thy destruction, hee will
accuse thee, mocking thy impietie, and God will leaue thee,
185 being more offended at thy neglect, or rather contempt of his
mercy, than at thy first offence.
Therefore runne quickly, esteeme no sin small, but what
member soeuer caused thee to offend him, bring it before him,
and let it assist thee chiefly in thy repentance. If thine eye teach
190 thee wantonnesse, couetousnesse, or the like, let them powre
forth teares to purchase thee a pardon. If thy tongue haue
offended toward God or thy neighbour, bring it with shame and
sorrow to confesse in priuate, what it was not ashamed to glory
of in publike. Learne to be ashamed to commit sinne, but, being
195 committed, hope not to hide it from God by any other meanes,
than by hearty repentance: so indeed thou maist winne his
mercy to couer thy transgression, and in his Sonnes passion he
will bury thine offences, so as hee will hide them from himselfe: but then thou must delay no time, goe quickly, get thee
200 alone, weare thy knees, wring thy hands, beat thy breast, know
as little measure in thy sorrow, as thou didst in thy sinne. The
Lord will not despise a contrite heart, and though hee let thee

kneele longe he will haue mercy at the last[.] learne of Iaⴖkob
to cry wth a feruent spirit[:] I will not let thee go except thou
blesse mee[.] our Sauior saythe[,] ye King^e^dom of heauen suf-
ferethe violence and the violent take it by force[.]

4

200   Thus you see it must bee an eager not a slothefull cours that
must bringe you to heauen: take heed thearfore that you auoyd
all the [k]indes of this sin[,] whatsoeuer you go about doo it wth
cheerfullnes[,] be ashamed of idlenes as thou art a man but
tremble at it as thou art a christian for be sure the diuell neuer
205   is so happy in his tentations as when he employs them on a
slothefull man whoo cannot endure to take so much payns as to
resist him[.]
      Salomon promises no other patrimony to A sluggard but
pouerty: God hates a slothefull [man.] witnes the 5 foolishe vir-
210   gins and the vnprofitable seruant Math: 25[,] the one christe
would not know[,] the other is branded wth too shamefull marks
< > ^euill^ and slothefull and his talent taken from him[.] what
more wretched estate can thear bee in the world: first to bee
hated of god as an idle drone not [f]it for his seruice: then
215   thorowgh extream pouerty to be contemned of all the world. Oh
then at no hand yeeld thy youth to slothe but so soon as thou
[hast] made thy prayr to god prepare to rise and risinge vse this
prayr[:]
      In thy name[,] oh blessed Sauior[,] I arise whoo wth the father
220   and the holy Spirit created me and wth thine own most precious
bloud hast redeemed mee: I beseech thee this day to gouern,
keep, and blesse me. lead mee forthe, in euery good way. thearin
direct, and confirm mee. and after this frayle and miserable life.
bringe me to that blessed life. wch hathe no end, for thy great
225   merit, and mercy sake:
                                                    Amen[.]

5

Thou art noe sooner broke out of the arms of slothe but pride

---

197 to] Wrestle with god And to   197 except] vnlesse   203 be ashamed of idlenes]
om.   209 a] the   216 thou] Thou hast   222 me] keepe and   222 good] God
225 mercy] Mercies

kneele long, hee will haue mercy at the last. Learne of *Iacob* to
wrestle with God, and to cry with a feruent spirit, I will not let
205   thee goe vnlesse thou blesse me.[1] Our Sauiour saith, The Kingdome of Heauen suffereth violence, and the violent take it by
force.[2]

4

Thus you see, it must be an eager, not a slothfull course, that
must bring you to Heauen. Take heed therefore that you auoid
210   all the kinds of this sinne. Whatsoeuer you goe about, doe it
with cheerefulnesse. Be ashamed of idlenesse, as thou art a
man, but tremble at it, as thou art a Christian. For bee sure the
deuill neuer is so happy in his tentations, as when hee emploies
them on a slothfull man, who cannot endure to take so much
215   paines as to resist him.

    Solomon promises no other patrimony to a sluggard but
pouerty. GOD hates the slothfull. Witnesse the fiue foolish Virgins, and the vnprofitable seruant, *Matth.* 25. The one Christ
would not know; the other is branded with two shamefull
220   markes, euill and slothfull, and his talent taken from him. What
more wretched estate can there be in the world? first to bee hated
of God as an idle Drone, not fit for his seruice: then through
extreme pouerty to bee contemned of all the world. Oh then at
no hand yeeld thy youth to sloth, but so soone as thou hast made
225   thy prayer to God, prepare to rise, and rising vse this Prayer.

    'In thy Name, Oh blessed Sauiour, I arise, who with the
Father, and the holy Spirit, created mee, and with thine own
most precious bloud hast redeemed mee. I beseech thee this
day, to gouerne, keepe, and blesse mee: lead mee forth in euery
230   good way, therein direct and confirme mee, and after this fraile
and miserable life, bring mee to that blessed life which hath no
end, for thy great merit and mercies sake. *Amen.* [']

5

Thou art no sooner broke out of the armes of sloth, but pride

---

1 Genesis 32.24–6
2 Matthew 11.12

steps in diligently waytinge to furnishe thee wth any vayn toy in
thy attire and though I beleeue theare are diuers sorts of pride
more pestilent to th<i>e soule then this of apparell, yet this is
230   enough dangerous and I am sure betrays a mans folly more then
any other for, is it not a monstrous thinge to see a man whome
god hathe created of an exc^e^llent form each part answeringe
the due proportion of another should by a fantasticall habit
make himselfe so vgly that one cannot find among all gods crea-
235   tures any thinge like him. one man though not resembling
another in shape or face yet for his rationall soule soule [sic] is
like another but theas fashionists Haue I feare changed theyr
reasonable souls for proud souls w^{th}out reason; could they els
[betake themselues] to theas apish fashions a[n]d apish
240   behauior, cringing, shrugginge, startinge, and playinge the foole
euery way, so that they may truly say when they are fashionable that they are not like other men: and I beleeue wise men
will not be sorry for it, for whoo would be like them[?] I desire
thee for godsake shun this vanyty whether thou be son or
245   daughter[,] if thou bee a daughter I confesse thy taske is harder
because thou art weaker and thy temptations to this vice
greater for thou shalt see those whoo perhaps thou wilt thinke
lesse able exallted far aboue thee in this [k]inde and it may bee
thou wilt desire to be like them if not to outgoe them[.] but
250   beleeue and remember that I tell thee[,] the end of all theas van-
itys is bitter as gall, oh the remembrance of misspent time;
when thou shall grow in years and haue attayned no higher
knowledge, then to dress thy selfe. when thou shalt see halfe
p^rhapps all thy time spent and that of all thou hast sowed thou
255   hast nothinge to reap but repentance[,] late repentance, how
wilt thou greeue[,] how wilt thou accuse one folly for bringinge
another and in thy memory cast ouer the cause of each misfortune [which] hathe befallen thee, till passing from one to
another at last thou findest thy corrupt will to be the first
260   cause[?] and then thou willt

---

231 for, is it] It is   **236** soule] *om.*   **239** to theas apish] deforme And transforme
themselues by These new fangled   **239** a[n]d] And   **240** foole] fantastiques   **245**
thou bee] *om.*   **247** whoo] whom   **247** wilt] Shalt   **249** if not to outgoe them]
om.   **252** higher] other   **256** bringinge] bringing In   **257–8** misfortune] Misfortune

steps in diligently, waiting to furnish thee with any vaine toy in
235   thy attire. And though I beleeue there are diuers sorts of pride
more pestilent to the soule than this of apparell, yet this is
enough dangerous, and I am sure betraies a mans folly more
than any other. Is it not a monstrous thing to see a man, whom
God hath created of an excellent forme, each part answering the
240   due proportion of another, should by a fantasticall habit make
himselfe so vgly, that one cannot finde amongst all Gods crea-
tures any thing like him? One man, though not resembling
another in shape or face, yet for his rationall soule is like
another: but these fashionists[1] haue (I feare) changed their rea-
245   sonable soules for proud soules without reason: could they else
deforme and transforme themselues by these new fangled fashions, and apish behauiour; crindging,[2] shrugging, starting, and
playing the fantastiques[3] euery way. So that they may truly say
when they are fashionable, that they are not like other men:
250   and I beleeue wise men will not be sorry for it. For who would
be like them?

I desire thee for Gods sake shunne this vanitie, whether thou
bee sonne or daughter. If a daughter, I confesse thy taske is
harder because thou art weaker, and thy temptations to this
255   vice greater, for thou shalt see those whom perhaps thou wilt
thinke less able, exalted farre aboue thee in this kinde, and it
may bee thou wilt desire to bee like them, if not to out-goe[4]
them. But beleeue and remember that I tell thee, the end of all
these vanities is bitter as gall.

260   Oh the remembrance of mis-spent time, when thou shalt
grow in yeeres, and haue attained no other knowledge, than to
dresse thy selfe. When thou shalt see halfe, perhaps all, thy
time spent, and that of all thou hast sowed, thou hast nothing
to reape but repentance, late repentance, how wilt thou grieue?
265   How wilt thou accuse one folly for bringing in another? and in
thy memory cast ouer the cause of each misfortune which hast
befallen thee, till passing from one to another, at last thou findest thy corrupt will to bee the first cause, and then thou wilt

---

1 fashionists: followers of fashion
2 crindging: behaving obsequiously, or bowing in an obsequious manner
3 fantastiques: those who wear extravagant clothing
4 out-goe: surpass

wth [g]reef enough perceyue that if thou hadst serued god when
thou seruedst thy fond desires thou hadst now had peace of
hart[.] god of mercy giue thee grace to remember him in the days
of thy youthe: Mistake me not nor giue your selfe leaue to take
265   too much liberty wth sayinge[,] my mother was too strict: noe I
am not, for I giue you leaue to follow modest fashions but not to
be a beginner of fashion< > nor would I haue you follow it till it
be generall so that in not dooinge as others doo you might
appear more singular then wise, but in one word this is all I
270   desire; that you will not set your hart on such fooleris, and you
shall see that this modest cariage will win you reputation and
loue wth the wise and vertuous sort[.]
        And once agayn remember how many hours mayst thou giue
to god wch if thou< > spendest in theas vanitis thou shalt neuer
275   bee able to make account of[,] if thou doest but endeuor to doo
well god will accept the will for the deed but if thou willfully
spend the morninge of thy time in theas vanitis god will not be
put of wth such rekonings but punishments will follow such as I
pray god thou mayst not pull vppon thee:
280   Yet alas this is but one sort of pride and so far from beeing
accounted a vice that if the time mends not before you com to
vnderstandinge you will hear a well drest woman (for that is y^e
stile of honor) more comended then a wise or learned or religious woman: and it may bee this may moue you to follow theyr
285   idlenes but when you haue any such desire draw your sellfe to
consider what maner of persons the comended and comenders
are and you shall finde them all of one batche such as beeinge
vayn themselues applaud it in others, but if you will desire prays
follow the example of those religious women whoos vertuous
290   fames time has not powr to race out, as deuout Anna whoo
serued the L: wth fastinge and prayr luke 2[,] iust Elizabet whoo
serued god wthout reproof: religious Ester whoo taught her
mayds to fast and pray Est. 4. 15. and the chast Susanna whoos
story I hope the strictest will allow for a worthy example[.]

---

263 god] the God   267 fashion] fashions   283 or learned] or honest   287 as] a
289 women] woman

with griefe enough perceiue, that if thou hadst serued God
270   when thou seruedst thy fond desires, thou hadst now had peace
of heart. The God of mercy giue thee grace to remember him in
the dayes of thy youth.

Mistake me not, nor giue your selfe leaue to take too much
liberty with saying, My mother was too strict. No, I am not, for
275   I giue you leaue to follow modest fashions, but not to be a
beginner of fashions: nor would I haue you follow it till it bee
generall; so that in not doing as others doe, you might appeare
more singular than wise: but in one word, this is all I desire,
that you will not set your heart on such fooleries,[1] and you shall
280   see that this modest carriage will win you reputation and loue
with the wise and vertuous sort.

And once againe, remember how many houres maist thou
giue to God, which if thou spendest in these vanities, thou shalt
neuer bee able to make account of. If thou dost but endeuour to
285   doe well, God will accept the will for the deed, but if thou wilfully spend the morning of thy time in these vanities, God will
not bee put off with such reckonings, but punishments will follow, such as I pray God thou maist not pull vpon thee.

Yet alas, this is but one sort of pride, and so farre from being
290   accounted a vice, that, if the time mends not before you come
to vnderstanding, you will heare a well drest woman, (for that is
the stile of honour) more commended than a wise or honest, or
religious woman. And it may bee, this may moue you to follow
their idlenes: but when you haue any such desire, draw your
295   selfe to consider what manner of persons the commended and
commenders are, and you shall finde them all of one batch,
such as being vaine themselues, applaud it in others.

But if you will desire praise, follow the example of those religious women, whose vertuous fames time hath not power to
300   raze out: as deuout *Anna*, who serued the Lord with fasting and
prayer, *Luke* 2. Iust *Elizabeth*, who serued God without
reproofe[2]: Religious *Ester*, who taught her Maids to fast and
pray, *Est.* 4. 15. and the chaste *Susanna*, whose story, I hope, the
strictest will allow for a worthy example.[3]

---

1 fooleries: foolish things
2 Luke 1.6
3 The story of Susanna appears in the Old Testament Apocryphal book of the
same name.

295   I am so fearfull thou shouldst fall into this sin that I could
spend my little time of life in exhortinge thee from it, I know it
is the most dangerous[,] subtle sin that can steale the hart of
man[,] it will allter shapes as oft as the chamelyon dothe
colors[,] it will fit it selfe to all dispositions and wch is most
300   strange it will so disguise it selfe that he must be cunninge
whoo discerns it from humility, nay it may ly in thine own hart
and if thou beest not a diligent searcher of thy selfe thou shalt
not know it, but, if thou watche well thou shallt take it for it
hathe one property that cannot change, as the comon people
305   beleeue the diuell cannot allter the shape of one foot[:] [i]t is
true of pride that though it bee transformed into ^that^ angell
of light humility, yet thou mayst know it by selfe loue, if thou
findest that wthin thee? be sure pride is not far of, for humility
will make the seem vilde in thyne own eys, it will make thee
310   see thine own faults and confess them, to be greater then other
mens, so that thou wilt respect euery man aboue thy selfe. but
the rules of selfe conceyt are iust contrary, they stand on tiptoes
rekoninge theyr vertues like the proud pharisee scorninge to
bee like other men. shun it for gods sake for if thou entertayn it
315   it is such a shameles flatterer that it will make thee beleeue
thou art greater[,] wiser[,] learneder [t]hen all the company
when indeed thou willt prooue thy selfe the greatest foole of
them wearyinge them all wth thy vayn talke, <of this vice> Salomon saythe[,] Pride goes before distruction and a hy   prov 16 18
320   minde before the fall and our blessed Sauiour the true
pattern of humility exhorts vs to learn of him that was lowly
and meek in hart and if wee do so hee promises wee   Ma 11 29
shall finde rest vnto our souls and he vses threatninge whear
perswasion will not serue[:] whoosoeuer exalltethe himselfe
325   shall bee humbled, read the holy scriptures often and   Lu 14 11
diligently and thou shalt finde continuall threatnings agaynst
pride[,] punishments of pride and warnings from pride, Thou
shalt finde no sin so heauyly punished as this[.] it made diuells
of angells, a beast of great Nabu-

---

295 fearfull] fearefull that   **303** but, if ... take it] *om.*   **306** transformed] Changed
309 thee] *om.*   **312–13** tiptoes rekoninge theyr] *om.*   **314** gods sake] thy soules
sake   **323** and he vses] Neither want there curses   **324** perswasion] perswasions
327 punishments] punishment

305   I am so fearefull that thou shouldst fall into this sinne, that I
could spend my little time of life in exhorting thee from it. I
know it is the most dangerous subtill sinne that can steale the
heart of man, it will alter shapes as oft as the Camelion doth
colours, it will fit it selfe to all dispositions, and (which is most
310   strange) it will so disguise it selfe, that he must be cunning who
discernes it from humilitie, nay it may lie in thine owne heart,
and if thou beest not a diligent searcher of thy selfe, thou shalt
not know it: but if thou watch well thou shalt take it, for it
hath one property that cannot change, as the common people
315   beleeue the Deuill cannot alter the shape of one foot. It is true
of pride, that though it bee changed into that Angell of light,
Humility, yet thou maist know it by self-loue; if thou findest
that within thee, be sure pride is not farre off. For humility will
make thee seeme vile in thine owne eyes, it will make thee see
320   thine owne faults, and confesse them to bee greater than other
mens, so that thou wilt respect euery man aboue thy selfe. But
the rules of selfe-conceit are iust contrary, they stand on tiptoes, reckning their vertues like the proud Pharisie,[1] scorning to
be like other men.

325   Shunne it for thy soules sake, for if thou entertaine it, it is
such a shamelesse flatterer, that it will make thee beleeue thou
art greater, wiser, learneder than all the company, when indeed,
thou wilt proue thy selfe the greatest foole of them, wearying
them all with thy vaine talke.

330   *Solomon* saith, *Pride goeth before destruction, Prou.* 16. 18.
And a high minde before the fall. And our blessed Sauiour, the
true patterne of humility, exhorts vs *to learne of him that was
lowly and meek in heart, Mat.* 11. 29. And if we doe so, he
promises we shall find rest vnto our soules. Neither want there
335   curses, threatning, where perswasions will not serue. Whosoeuer exalteth himselfe shall bee humbled, *Luke* 14. 11. Reade
the holy Scriptures often and diligently, and thou shalt finde
continuall threatnings against pride, punishment of pride, and
warnings from pride. Thou shalt finde no sinne so heauily pun-
340   ished as this: it made Deuils of Angels,[2] a beast of great *Nabu-*

---

1 Luke 18.10–14

2 it made Deuils of Angels: the fall of Lucifer and his angelic followers prior to the
creation of the world

330 chodonezer, doggs meat of Iesabell, and I will conclude wth a
     good mans sayinge[:] if all the sins rayg< >ninge in the world
     weare burnt to ashes euen the ashes of pride would bee able to
     produce them all agayn[.]
        I know in fewer words thear might much more haue bin sayd
335 agaynst this sin but <not w^thstanding> I know not whoo will
     say so much to thee when I am gon, thearfore I desire thou
     mayst bee taught theas my instructions when thou art young
     that this foule sin [m]ay bee weeded out before it take deep root
     in thy hart[.]
340   I will return now to my first purpose wch is to set thee down
     one day for a pattern how I would haue thee spend all the days
     of thy life[.]

     6

     Thearfore auoydinge all maner of pride make thy selfe decently
     ready wch beeinge don retire to a place alone whear humblinge
345 thy selfe vppon thy knees agayn renew thy prayrs humbly con-
     fessinge and earnestly desiringe forgiuenes for all thy sins and
     vse Dr Smiths morninge prayr: then wch I know not a better nor
     did I euer finde more comfort in any: <th> in aduising you to A
     set form of prayr I do not prohibit conceyved prayr but humbly
350 beg of god to giue you grace to pray often out of your own medi-
     tatyons accordinge to his will[,] but when it shall pleas god to
     call you to the charge of a family I will not direct but deliuer my
     opinion, that then a set form of prayr is most necessary, my rea-
     son is that your seruants beeinge vsed to it are allways ready to
355 go alonge wth you word for word as you pray and continuance
     makes them to vnderstand euery word wch must needs cause
     greater deuotion.

     7

     when you haue finished your priuate prayr be sure that you

---

333 produce] Reduce   342 life] liue   348 did I euer] Euer did I   355 wth you] with
you In their hearts   357 deuotion] deuotion and giue more life to the prayers

chodonezzar,[1] dogs meat of *Iezabel*,[2] and I will conclude with a
good mans saying, If all the sinnes reigning in the world were
burnt to ashes, euen the ashes of pride would bee able to reduce
them all againe.

345   I know in fewer words there might much more haue beene
said against this sinne, but I know not who will say so much to
thee when I am gone. Therefore I desire thou maist bee taught
these my instructions when thou art young, that this foule
sinne may be weeded out before it take deepe root in thy heart.

350   I will returne now to my first purpose, which is to set thee
downe one day for a patterne, how I would haue thee spend all
the dayes of thy life.

6

Therefore auoiding all manner of pride, make thy selfe
decently ready, which being done, retire to a place alone, where

355   humbling thy selfe vpon thy knees, againe renew thy prayers,
humbly confessing, and earnestly desiring forgiuenesse for all
thy sinnes, and vse Doctor *Smiths* morning prayer,[3] than which
I know not a better, nor euer did I finde more comfort in any.

In aduising you to a set forme of prayer, I doe not prohibit

360   conceiued Prayer, but humbly beg of God to giue you grace to
pray often out of your owne meditations according to his will.

But when it shall please God to call you to the charge of a
family, I will not direct, but deliuer my opinion, that then a set
forme of prayer is most necessary: my reason is, that your ser-

365   uants being vsed to it, are alwayes ready to goe along with you
in their hearts, word for word, as you pray, and continuance[4]
makes them to vnderstand euery word, which must needs cause
greater deuotion, and giue more life to the prayers.

7

When you haue finished your priuate prayer, be sure that you

---

1 *Nabuchodonezzar*: Daniel 5.21
2 *Iezabel*: 1 Kings. 9.10, 36, 2 Kings 21.23
3 Doctor *Smiths* morning prayer: Henrie Smith, *Three Prayers, one for the Morning, another for the Euening: the third for a sick-man*, sig. A2–6
4 continuance: persistence

absent not your selfe from [p]ublick prayr if it bee vsed in the
360   house whear you liue wch ended go and vse any lawfull recreatyon eyther for thy profit or plesure and from all theas exercises reserue A time to sit down to som good study but vse that
most that may make thee greatest; diuinity: it will make thee
greater[,] richer[,] happyer then the greatest kingedom of the
365   earthe though thou couldst posses it[,] if any man serue mee[,]
saythe christ[,] him will my father Honor, if Mardochey wear
^thought^ so highly honored by Ahashuerous for a little gay
trappinge what shall bee don to him whoom god will honor[?]
thearfore if thou desirest honor serue the L: and thou art sure of
370   it, if riches be thy aym St Paul assures thee that godlynes is
great gayn[,] if thou couet plesure set Dauids delight before
thine eys: I haue had more delight in thy testimonys then in all
maner of riches Ps Cxix and in the 92 Ps: he saythe[,] thou L:
hast made mee glad by thy works[,] in the 4 Psal: Thou hast
375   giuen mee more Ioy of hart &: and readinge the 91 Psal[:] thou
shalt see what maner of blessings they are that god makes his
chilldren merry wthall[.] and when thou hast once fixt thy hart
to thi[s] study it will be so sweet that the more thou learnest
the more thou willt desire and the more thou desirest the more
380   god will loue the[.] thou willt study to [so] well in priuat and
practis it in all thy actions publickly[,] thou will weygh thy
thoughts so euen that thy words shall not bee light and a few
lines I will vse to perswade thee to be aduised in thy words[.]

8

Though it is as much to say [,] Remember thy creator when
385   thou speakest[,] as if I could vse all ye exhortatyons and tell thee
all ye perills y^t belongs to speech yet so apt are wee to forget god
in our foolishe taulke that somtimes wee by our discours would
make gods of our selues[,] thearfore it will not bee amiss to
receyue a few instructyons though weak from me for orderinge
390   thy speech[.]

370 absent not your selfe from publike prayer, if it bee vsed in the
house where you liue: which ended, goe and vse any lawfull
[re]creation, either for thy profit or pleasure, and from all these
exercises reserue a time to sit downe to some good study, but
vse that most that may make thee greatest, Diuinitie. It will
375 make thee greater, richer, happier than the greatest Kingdome
of the earth, though thou couldst possesse it. If any man serue
me, saith Christ, him will my father honor[1]; If *Mordecay* were
thought so highly honoured by *Ahasuerus* for a little gay trap-
ping,[2] what shall be done to him whom God will honour?
380   Therefore if thou desirest honour, serue the Lord, and thou
art sure of it. If riches bee thy aime, Saint *Paul* assures thee,
that *Godlinesse is great gaine*.[3] If thou couet pleasure, set
Dauids delight before thine eies, *I haue had more delight in thy
testimonies than in all manner of riches, Psal.* 119. And in the
385 92. Psalme hee saith, *Thou Lord hast made mee glad by thy
workes.* In the 4. Psalme, *Thou hast giuen mee more ioy of
heart, &c.* and reading the 91. Psalme, thou shalt see what manner of blessings they are that God makes his children merry
withall. And when thou hast once fixt thy heart to this study, it
390 will be so sweet, that the more thou learnest, the more thou
wilt desire, and the more thou desirest, the more God will loue
thee. Thou wilt study so well in priuate, and practise it in all
thy actions publikely, thou wilt weigh thy thoughts so euen,
that thy words shall not bee light, and a few lines I will vse to
395 perswade thee to bee aduised in thy words.

8

    Though it is as much to say, Remember thy Creator when
thou speakest, as if I could vse all the exhortations, and tell thee
all the perils that belong to speech, yet so apt are wee to forget
God in our foolish talke, that sometimes wee by our discourse
400 would make Gods of our selues. Therefore it will not bee
amisse to receiue a few instructions, though weake, from mee
for ordering thy speech.

---

1 John 12.26
2 Ester 8.15
3 1 Timothy 6.6

The morninge I haue dedicated to <p>meditatyon[,] <good study> prayr[,] good studys and honest recreatyon: The noon time is most vsed for discours it beeing all a man can doo while he eats [a]nd it is a time whearin a man ought to bee carefull of
395   his speech hauinge before him gods good blessings to refreshe his< > body and honest company to <refresh> ^recreate^ his minde[.] Thearfore [he] ought to be no way offensiue in his speech eyther to god or good men, but most especially take heed that neyther heedlesnes nor earnestnes in thy discours
400   caus thee to take gods holy name in vayn but allways speake of him wth reuerence and vnderstandinge; next let not thy neygh-bor suffer in thy speech but be rather silent then speake ill of any man though he deserue it and that thou mayst doo thus obserue this rule[:] whensoeuer thou hearest one ill spoken of
405   before [t]hou second it examin thine own hart and it is odds but thou mayst finde in thy selfe eyther ye same fault or a worse then that hee is accused for; so thou shalt be forced eyther to mend thy selfe or not to <accuse> ^condem^ him: allso shun multiplicity of words and what thou speakest be sure to vnder-
410   stand fully for it is a gratinge to the ear to heare a man talke at random, if thou desirest to better thy selfe; modestly aske a question of those whom thou seest haue knowledge to resolue thee and bee lesse ashamed to confess thy ignorance then by houldinge a foolish argument, to betray it. and euer auoyd that
415   scornfull fashyon of questioninge [a] man whoo thou knowest cannot make thee a satisfyinge answear[,] neyther make a scorn of his ignorance for bee assured he knows somthinge that thou doest not know[.]
         If god haue giuen thee a ready wit take heed thou abuse it
420   not[,] at no time mayntaine arguments agaynst the truthe for it is hard to do it w^thout offendinge the god of truthe, and by it, thou maist harm thy weake brother, but the greatest harm will bee thine own when thou comst to giue account for thy idle words; in thy mirthe shun suche iestinge as may make thee
425   offensiue[,]

---

412 seest] seest to   415 questioninge] questioning a   420 truthe] truth especially In sacred or morall matter

The morning I haue dedicated to meditation, praier, good
studies, and honest recreation. The noone time is most vsed for
405   discourse, it beeing all a man can doe while hee eats, and it is a
time wherein a man ought to bee carefull of his speech, hauing
before him Gods good blessings to refresh his body, and honest
company to recreate his minde, and therefore ought to bee no
way offensiue in his speech either to God or good men. But
410   most especially take heed that neither heedlesnesse nor ear-
nestnesse in thy discourse, cause thee to take Gods holy Name
in vaine, but alwaies speake of him with reuerence and vnderstanding.

Next, let not thy neighbour suffer in thy speech, but bee
415   rather silent than speake ill of any man, though hee deserue it.
And that thou maist doe thus, obserue this rule; whensoeuer
thou hearest one ill spoken of, before thou second it, examine
thine owne heart, and it is ods but[1] thou maist finde in thy selfe
either the same fault, or a worse than that hee is accused for. So
420   thou shalt bee forced either to mend thy selfe, or not to condemne him.

Also shunne multiplicity of words, and what thou speakest,
bee sure to vnderstand fully, for it is a grating to the eare to
heare a man talke at randome. If thou desirest to better thy
425   selfe, modestly aske a question of those whom thou seest to
haue knowledge to resolue[2] thee, and bee lesse ashamed to confesse thy ignorance, than by holding a foolish argument, to
betray it. And euer auoid that scornfull fashion of questioning a man, who, thou knowest, cannot make thee a satisfying
430   answer: neither make a scorne of his ignorance, for bee assured
hee knowes something that thou dost not know.

If God haue giuen thee a ready wit, take heed thou abuse it
not. At no time maintaine arguments against the truth, especially in sacred or morall matter: for it is hard to doe it, without
435   offending the God of truth; and by it thou maist harme thy
weake brother, but the greatest harme will bee thine owne
when thou commest to giue account for thy idle words.

In thy mirth shun such iesting as may make thee offensiue,

---

1 it is ods but: it is probable that
2 resolue: answer

scoffinge becoms not a christian[.] prise not thearfore the frothe
of an Idle wit before the faythe of a vertuous frend: and I pray
thee as thou wouldst haue < > blessings mulltiplyed vppon thee
let noe [s]peech passe from thee that may greeue chast ears[,]
430   how hatefull is obscean speech in rude people? but it makes one
of gentile birthe odious to all honest company[.] Salomon says[,]
A wise man conceals knowledge but the hart of a foole pub-
lishethe foolishnes Pro 12 23 and he that keepethe his mouthe
keepethe his life 13. 3. and in the 14. 3. the lips of the wise pre-
435   serue them[.]
     to conclude let thy tonge and thy hart go together[,] hate dis-
simulation and lyinge and god will loue thee wch I humbly beg
of him::: 3–
<If t>

9

440   If th<y>ou ^keep thy^ thoughts < > holy and thy words pure I
shall not need to feare but all thy actions will bee honest yet
my fear thou shouldst know the way ánd <yet> go aside will not
suffer my councell to leaue thee alone till thou com to thy iour-
neys end: first then bee carefull when thou art alone that thou
445   doo nothinge that thou wouldest not doo if men saw thee
rememberin[g] that gods ey is allways open, and thyne own conscience will bee witnes enough agaynst thee[.] next be sure that
no action of thine may bee a scandall to thy profession[,] I mean
to the professyon of the true religion[,] this indeed is as much as
450   to say to thee[,] eschue euill: for thear is not the least sin thou
canst doo but the enemis of truthe ^will^ be glad to say[:] loe
this is one of them that professes god in his mouthe but see
what his life is; thearfore a great care ought a christian to haue
especially those whome god has set as lights in his churche[.]
455   whatsoeuer thou art about to doo examin it by gods comandements[,] if it bee agreeable to them; go on cheerfully and though
the end answear not thy hopes neuer greeue nor grudge but be
glad that gods will is performed and let thy

---

scoffing becomes not a Christian. Prise not[1] therefore the froth
440   of an idle wit, before the faith of a vertuous friend.

And I pray thee, as thou wouldest haue blessings multiplied
vpon thee, let no speech passe from thee that may grieue chaste
eares. How hatefull is obscene speech in rude people? But it
makes one of gentle birth odious to all honest company. *Solo-*
445   *mon* saies, A wise man conceales knowledge, but *the heart of a*
foole publisheth foolishnesse, Prou. 12. 23. and *hee that keep-*
eth his mouth, keepeth his life, 13. 3. and in the 14. 5. *The lips*
of the wise preserue them.

To conclude, let thy tongue and thy heart goe together, hate
450   dissimulation and lying, and God will loue thee, which I humbly beg of him.

9

If thou keepe thy thoughts holy, and thy words pure, I shall
not need to feare, but all thy actions will bee honest. But my
feare thou shouldest know the way, and yet goe aside, will not
455   suffer my counsell to leaue thee alone, till thou come to thy
iournies end.

First then bee carefull when thou art alone, that thou doe
nothing that thou wouldest not doe if men saw thee: remember
that Gods eye is alwayes open, and thine owne conscience will
460   bee witnesse enough against thee.

Next bee sure that no action of thine may bee a scandall to
thy profession, I meane to the profession of the true Religion.
This indeed is as much as to say to thee, Eschew euill. For there
is not the least sinne thou canst doe, but the enemies of truth
465   will bee glad to say, Loe, this is one of them that professes God
in his mouth, but see what his life is. Therefore a great care
ought a Christian to haue, especially those whom God hath set
as lights in his Church.

Whatsoeuer thou art about to doe, examine it by Gods Com-
470   mandements: if it bee agreeable to them, goe on cheerefully,
and though the end answer not thy hopes, neuer grieue nor
grudge, but bee glad that Gods will is performed, and let thy

---

1 Prise not: care nothing for

trust in him assuer thee that all things work together for the
460   best to them that loue god, and though it appear a crosse be
assured it is a blessinge[.] therefore make right vse of it, examin
thy selfe what sin thou hast comitted that may chalenge that
punishment, repent it and reconcile god vnto thee bearing thy
cross wth patience, and dou[bt] not, he that depriued thee of thy
465   hope to try thee: will ([i]f thou bear it well) < > ^giue^ th<y>ee
as great or a greater blessinge then thou hopedst for[.]
    But if thou shallt finde that thy attempts will not endure that
tryall break from them and tell the diuell in playn tearms thou
hast a light to discern his snares by and thearfore scornst to bee
470   his slaue; for beleeue me my childe if thou shalt out of any
worldly respect doo a dishonest act it may bee thou mayst
thriue in it a while but the end is miserable[.] oh the burden of a
wounded conscience whoo can beare: if thou seest others thriue
and grow great in suche courses; read the 73 Psalm[,] thear thou
475   shallt see Dauid himselfe confesses his [f]oot had wellnigh slipt
when hee saw the prosperyty of the wicked[,] he describes all
theyr felicitys but at the last when he went into the sanctuary
he found what theyr end was[,] how they wear set in slippery
places &- and then hee cryes[,] whoom haue I in heauen but
480   thee, and I haue desired non in the earthe wth thee[.] Alas all
theyr labor is but to build a paper house vppon the sand w^{ch}
though it bee neuer so glorious to look vppon a small tempest
will shatter it: when if thou lay the foundatyon of thy happines
vppon christ< > the rock of thy salluatyon and build it wth
485   zelous seruice of him accordinge to truthe then though the
flouds beat [a]gaynst it and huge tempests threaten it thou
needest not fear for thy walls will stand fast and thy foundatyon
will secure thee[.] it wear enough to perswade any man to be
honest if he would consider the day of affliction and store vp
490   the comfort of a quiet conscience agaynst it came[,] for only
that discerns the patient Iob from dispayringe kayn. Kayn hideously cryes out his punishment is greater then hee can beare:
Iob sighs forthe[,] Loe: though hee slay me yet will I trust in
him: indeed till

---

463 repent] Repent of   479 &-] om.   487 foundatyon] foundations

trust in him assure thee, that all things worke together for the
best to them that loue GOD. And though it appeare a crosse, be
475   assured it is a blessing. Therefore make right vse of it; examine
thy selfe what sinne thou hast committed that may challenge
that punishment, repent of it, and reconcile God vnto thee,
bearing thy Crosse with patience, and doubt not hee that depriued thee of thy hope to try thee, will (if thou beare it well) giue
480   thee as great or a greater blessing than thou hopest for. But if
thou shalt finde that thy attempts will not endure that triall,
breake from them, and tell the Deuill in plaine termes thou
hast a light to discerne his snares by, and therefore scornest to
be his slaue. For beleeue mee, my childe, if thou shalt out of
485   any worldly respect doe a dishonest act, it may bee thou maist
thriue in it a while, but the end is miserable. Oh the burthen of
a wounded conscience who can beare?

If thou seest others thriue & grow great in such courses, reade
the 73. Psalme; there thou shalt see *Dauid* himselfe confesses
490   his foot had wel-nigh slipt when hee saw the prosperity of the
wicked: Hee describes all their felicities, but at the last when
hee went into the Sanctuary, hee found what their end was,
how they were set in slippery places, &c. and then hee cries,
Whom haue I in Heauen but thee? And I haue desired none in
495   *the earth with thee.* Alas, all their labour is but to build a paper
house vpon the sand, which though it bee neuer so glorious to
looke vpon, a small tempest will shatter it. When if thou lay the
foundation of thy happinesse vpon Christ the rocke of thy saluation, and build it with zealous seruice of him according to
500   truth, then though the flouds beat against it, and huge tempests
threaten it, thou needest not feare, for thy wals will stand fast,
and thy foundations will secure thee.[1]

It were enough to perswade any man to bee honest if hee
would consider the day of affliction, and store vp the comfort of
505   a quiet conscience against it came: for onely that discernes the
patient *Iob* from despairing *Caine*. *Caine* hideously cries out,
his punishment is greater than hee can beare. *Iob* sighs forth,
Loe though hee slay mee, yet will I trust in him.[2] Indeed, till

---

1 Matthew 7.24–7
2 Job 13.15

495 affliction coms the worser sort of men appear to be the happiest
but then the chaf is soon known from the wheat[,] the good man
knows his cross is good for him[,] bears it patiently and casts his
care on christ[,] his hart knows no repininge, nor his tonge other
complayninge but[,] shall I receyue good from god and not euill:
500 on the contrary when affliction falls vppon those whoo haue
layd thear foundatyon on the sand alas they haue noe comfort[,]
they are eyther ashamed or besotted[,] they cannot finde god[,]
nay they will not seek him but instead of seekinge councell
from him they are not ashamed (wth forsaken Saule) to implore
505 the diuell[.] what do they less that seek after witches for lost
goods[,] cure for themselues[,] theyr children or cattell: I hope
there are but few of theas but I know whear god is once forsaken, man is apt to fall into the depthe of sin[.] it is grace[,]
mear grace[,] that preserues gods chilldren from theas dangerous
510 falls wch grace I beseech allmighty god make vs all partakers of,
and to conclude how I would haue thee square [thy] actions[,]
whatsoeuer thou doest remember thou art in the presence of
god (whoo will expect an account from thee) so thou willt not
dare to doo euill and thou willt doo well chearfully becaus thou
515 art sure it pleses th<y>e Lord whoo sees thy willingnes and will
not leaue thee vnrewarded: the vices most raygning in theas
[times] I must particularly aduise thee ^to^ shun[.] first
swearinge[,] for god sake let your comunicatyon be yea[,] yea
and nay[,] nay: for what is more[,] saythe christ[,] comethe of
520 euill, keep not company wth a swearer lest custom make thee
forget how great the sin is and so by little and little thou mayst
get thy selfe a habit of it[.] reprooue it in thy frend if he will
brook reprooff, but it is to no end to reprooue a scorner[:]
[r]ebuke not a scorner lest hee hate thee but rebuke a wise man
525 and hee will loue thee: Prov: 9. 8.
allways keep a watche before thine own lips and remember
that thou needest not swear if thou doest not accustom thy

---

507 theas] those   510 w^ch] of which   510 of] om.   511 square] s<>quare thine   512
remember] Remember that   516 theas] these times   523–4 but it … [r]ebuke not] om.

affliction comes, the worser sort of men appeare to bee the hap-
510 piest, but then the chaffe is soone knowne from the wheat: the
good man knowes his crosse is good for him, beares it patiently;
and casts his care on Christ, his heart knowes no repining, nor
his tongue other complaining, but *Shall I receiue good from
God and not euill?*[1]
515 On the contrary, when affliction fals vpon those who haue
laid their foundation on the sand, alas, they haue no comfort,
they are either ashamed or besotted,[2] they cannot finde God,
nay they will not seeke him: but in stead of seeking counsell
from him, they are not ashamed (with forsaken *Saul*) to implore
520 the Deuill.[3] What doe they lesse that seeke after Witches for
lost goods, cure for themselues, their children, or cattell? I hope
there are but few of these: but I know where God is once forsaken, man is apt to fall into the depth of sinne. It is grace,
meere grace, that preserues Gods children from these dangerous
525 fals, of which grace I beseech Almighty God make vs all partakers.
And to conclude, how I would haue thee square thine actions,
whatsoeuer thou doest, remember that thou art in the presence
of God, (who will expect an account from thee) so thou wilt not
530 dare to doe euill, and thou wilt doe well cheerefully, because
thou art sure it pleases the Lord, who sees thy willingnesse, and
will not leaue thee vnrewarded.
The vices most reigning in these times I must particularly
aduise thee to shun: first, swearing. For Gods sake, let your
535 communication be yea, yea, and nay, nay, for what is more
(saith Christ) commeth of euill.[4] Keepe not company with a
swearer, lest custome make thee forget how great the sin is, and
so by little and little thou maist get thy selfe a habit of it.
Reproue it in thy friend, if hee will brooke reproofe: but it is to
540 no end to reproue a scorner: Rebuke not a scorner lest hee hate
thee, but rebuke a wise man, and he will loue thee, *Prou. 9. 8.*
Alwayes keepe a watch before thine owne lips, and remember
that thou needest not sweare if thou doest not accustome thy

---

1 Job 2.10
2 besotted: stupified
3 1 Samuel 28.6–7
4 Matthew 5.37

selfe to ly for if thou vsest to tell truthes thy word will be as
current as thy oathe[.] I hope thy callinge if god haue made thee
530   [a] man will bee of authority to reproue this vice in others and
not to delight in it thy selfe[.] if thou beest a daughter thou hast
. a callinge to wch thou must not dishonor[,] thou art a christian
and christ comands thou shouldst not swear at all. Mat. 5. 34.
beside thou art a mayd and such ought thy modesty to be that
535   thou shouldst scars speak but when thou answerest[,] thou that
art young speak if need bee and yet scarsely when thou art twise
Asked Eccle: 32 8[.]

    The next vice too to comon in this age is Drunkennes wch is
the highway to hell[,] a man may trauayl in it from sin to sin till
540   the diuell show him he can go no farther as a trauayler from in
to in till hee com to his Iorneys end[,] oh thin[k] how filthy is
that sin that makes a man a beast all his life and a diuell at his
deathe[.] Salomon asks[,] to whom is woe[,] to whom is sorrow[,]
to who[m] is strife[,] to whom is murmuringe[,] to whom are
545   wounds wthout caus and to whom is rednes of the eys[?] and in
the next verse answears[,] euen to them that tarry longe at the
wine and to the end of the chapter sets forthe the miseris occasioned by this vice Pro: 23[.] that thou maist auoyd this sin be
carefull in the choyce of thy frends for it is they that ^will^
550   betray < >^thee^ to this sin[,] neuer make choyce of a drunkard
to thy companyon [m]uch lesse thy {57} frend for our
kinged^om^ hathe of late afforded more examples of those
whoo haue bin slayn by theyr frends in a drunken quarrell then
those that haue fallen by the enemis sword and how vnfit is he
555   to be a frend that when thou shallt haue need of his councell
will haue his head instead of wisdom fild wth wine and ad rather
greef then comfort to thy nesessitis[?] and agayn what secret
thou shalt trust him wth thou maist be sure shall bee vomited
forthe and all thy comfort must bee he did it vnwillingly when
560   hee knew not what he did[.] thus thou seest to bee a drunkard is
to be a man vnfit for gods seruice or good mens company[,] I
beseech god giue thee grace to detest it[.]

---

529 thee] ^thee a^   531–7 thou hast ... 32 8] Remember thou art A Maid and such
ought thy Modesty to bee that thou shouldest scarce speak but when thou Answerest
thou art young speake I need bee and yet scarcely when thou art twice asked Eccles
32: 8: whatsoeuer thou bee thou hast A calling which thou Must not dishonour
thou art A christian and christ commands thou shalt not sweare at all Mat 5: 34
551 57] *om.*

545 selfe to lie. For if thou vsest to tell truths, thy word will bee as currant[1] as thy oath. I hope thy calling (if God hath made thee a man) will bee of authority to reproue this vice in others, and not to delight in it thy selfe. If thou beest a Daughter, remember thou art a Maid, and such ought thy modesty to bee, that thou shouldest scarce speak, but when thou answerest: thou art

550 young, speake if need bee, and yet scarcely when thou art twice asked, *Eccles*. 32. 8. Whatsoeuer thou bee, thou hast a calling which thou must not dishonour: thou art a Christian, and Christ commaunds thou shalt not sweare at all, *Mat*. 5. 34.

The next vice too too common in this age is Drunkennesse,

555 which is the high way to hell: a man may trauell in it from sinne to sinne, till the Deuill shew him hee can goe no further, as a Traueller from Inne to Inne, till hee come to his iourneyes end. Oh thinke how filthy is that sinne that makes a man a beast all his life, and a Deuill at his death. *Solomon* askes, To whom is

560 woe? to whom is sorrow? to whom is strife? to whom is murmuring? to whom are wounds without cause? and to whom is rednesse of the eies? And in the next verse answers, Euen to them that tarry[2] long at the Wine, and to the end of the Chapter, sets forth the miseries occasioned by this vice, *Prou*. 23.

565 That thou maist auoid this sinne, be carefull in the choise of thy friends, for it is they that will betray thee to this sinne. Neuer make choice of a Drunkard to thy companion, much lesse thy friend. For our Kingdome hath of late afforded more examples of those who haue beene slaine by their friends in a

570 drunken quarrell, than those that haue fallen by the enemies sword: and how vnfit is hee to bee a friend, that when thou shalt haue need of his counsell, will haue his head, in stead of wisdome, fild with wine, and adde rather griefe than comfort to thy necessities? And againe, what secret thou shalt trust him

575 with, thou maist bee sure shall be vomited forth, and all thy comfort must bee, He did it vnwillingly, when hee knew not what hee did. Thus thou seest to bee a Drunkard, is to bee a man vnfit for Gods seruice, or good mens company. I beseech God giue thee grace to detest it.

---

1 currant: current, accepted as geniune
2 tarry: continue, linger

   Next I must exhort thee from a sin that I cannot name[.] thou
must search thine own hart for it, it is thy da^r^linge sin that
565   wch too enioy thou couldst resist all others[,] at least thou
thinkest so; but do not harbor it[,] search diligently for it in thy
own nature and when thou hast found it cast it headlong from
thee[.] it is thy souls subtle betrayer and all thy other sins
depend vppon it[,] theare is not so much danger in all the rest
570   that thou contendest wth as in this one that thou art lothe to
call a sin[,] thy other sins are like a rebellious multitude in a
comon wealthe wch wantinge a head doo little harm[,] this is
theyr head[,] cut it of and thou shalt see ^all^ th< >y other sins
dispearsed as an army of fearfull rebells when they hear theyr
575   great leaders head has kist the block[.] <Thus hauing spent the>

10

when thou hast spent the day in religious and honest exercises
in the eueninge return agayn to som good meditatyon or study
wch conclude wth prayr comendinge thy selfe to god and so shalt
thou ioyfully go to thy supper wch don and the time of rest com
580   as thou begannest in the morninge so shut vp the day wth humble thanksgiuinge for all the benefits that day receaued[,] harty
repentance for all thy sins comitted naming and bewaylinge
them[,] for [t]hou knowest not if thou repentest not to night
whether thou shallt liue to morrow and though thou weart sure
585   of it yet the oftner thou makest euen thy accounts wth god thy
sleeps will bee the sounder and thou shalt awake wth a hart full
of ioy and ready to serue the Lord: last comit thy selfe and all
that is thine to god in zealous praire vsinge Dr Smiths euening
prayr as his morninge[,] bothe wch though ^they^ bee for a fam-
590   ily yet are they easyly reduced too a priuat mans prayr: so
goinge to bed take thy rest beginning and endinge in him that is
both first and last: thus spend the 6 days thou hast to labor in,
that thou mayst bee redy to celebrate the Saboath to wch thear
belongs another {remember} [.]

---

565 thou couldst resist all others] *om.*   **584** liue] liue to repen^t^   **594** remember] *om.*

580   Next, I must exhort thee from a sinne, that I cannot name, thou must search thine owne heart for it. It is thy darling sin, that which to enioy, thou couldst resist all others, at least thou thinkest so. But doe not harbour it, search diligently for it in thine owne nature, and when thou hast found it, cast it head-
585 long from thee. It is thy soules subtill betraier, and all thy other sins depend vpon it. There is not so much danger in all the rest that thou contendest with, as in this one, that thou art loth to call a sinne. Thy other sinnes are like a rebellious multitude in a common wealth, which wanting a head, doe little harme.
590 This is their head, cut it off, and thou shalt see all thy other sins dispersed, as an army of fearfull Rebels, when they heare their greate leaders head hath kist the blocke.

    10

    When thou hast spent the day in religious and honest exer-cises, in the euening returne againe to some good meditation or
595 study, which conclude with prayer, commending thy selfe to God, and so shalt thou ioyfully goe to thy supper; which done, and the time of rest come, as thou begannest in the morning, so shut vp the day with humble thanksgiuing for all the benefits that day receiued, hearty repentance for all thy sinnes commit-
600 ted, naming and bewailing them. For thou knowest not if thou repentest not to night, whether thou shalt liue to repent to morrow. And though thou wert sure of it, yet the oftner thou makest euen thy accounts with God, thy sleepes will bee the sounder, and thou shalt awake with a heart full of ioy, and ready
605 to serue the Lord.
    Last, commit thy selfe, and all that is thine, to God in zealous Prayer, vsing Doctor *Smiths* euening prayer,[1] as his morning: both which though they be for a family, yet are they easily reduced to a priuate mans prayer. So going to bed, take thy rest,
610 beginning and ending in him who is both first and last. Thus spend the six dayes thou hast to labour in, that thou maist bee ready to celebrate the Sabbath, to which there belongs another *Remember*.

---

1 Doctor *Smiths* euening prayer: Smith, sigs. A6–B1ᵛ

11

595 Remember that thou keep holy the Sabathe day[.] this duty so
      often and earnestly comanded by god himselfe[,] so strictly ob-
      serued by the Iews (whoo that day might kindell noe fire nor vse
      any labor insomuch that the L: whoo is the god ^of^ mercy him
      selfe comanded the man that gathered sticks on that day to be
600 stoned): and a long time after zealously kept by the christians
      yet in theas days as if wee neyther had part in the creation nor
      redemption of the world wee keep noe sabboath or ^at^ the most
      but a shadow of a sabbathe[.] whear allmost can wee finde one
      that will loose a good bargayn rather then make it on the Lords
605 day or that will bridle his own desires to sanctify that day[?]
      truly thear are so few that it is hard to instance one: seeinge
      thearfore this danger in< > wch thou mayst easily bee intrapped
      by [t]he Diuells subtelty and followinge the multitude I cannot
      but wth all my powr exhort thee carefully to keep the Sabathe to
610 wch end I pray thee mark well the 4th comandement[:]
          Remember that thou keep holy the Sabathe day: 6 days shallt
      thou labor and doo all thou hast to doo: but ye seuenthe is the
      sabathe of the Lord thy God[,] in it thou shallt doo noe maner of
      work[,] thou[,] nor thy son[,] nor thy daughter[,] thy man ser-
615 uant[,] nor thy mayd seruant[,] nor thy cattell[,] nor the stranger
      that is w^thin thy gates[,] for in 6 days the Lord made Heauen and
      earthe[,] the sea and all that is thearin and rested the 7th day
      whearfore ye L blessed the 7th day and Hallowed it:
          If thou willt be won to the due obseruatyon of this day < > [as]
620 an obedient seruant? see god comands[,] Remember that thou
      keep holy the Sabbathe[,] if as a louinge and dutyfull son see
      how god perswades thee by reason[,] hee hathe giuen thee 6
      days to do thine own works and hee requires but one of thee[.]
      what canst thou say for thy ^selfe^[,] why thou shouldest not
625 wholy that day giue thy selfe to his seruice[?] lastly if thou willt

595 the Sabathe day[.] this] *om.*   596–600 so strictly … the christians] In the ould testament so confirmed to vs in the new by the Resurrection of our sauiour In Memory
whereof It Is called the lords day and perpetuall celebrated by the church   602 wee]
too many   606 truly thear … instance one] *om.*   615 nor the stranger] *om.*   619 day]
day as   622 god] god commands Remember that thou keepe holy the Sabbath day If
as a louing and dutiefull Sonne see how god   622 reason] Equitie grounded vpon his
owne bountie to thee

11

Remember that thou keep holy the Sabbath day. This duty so
often and earnestly commanded by GOD himselfe in the old
Testament, so confirmed to vs in the new, by the Resurrection
of our Sauiour, in memory whereof it is called the Lords day,
and perpetually celebrated by the Church, yet in these dayes, as
if wee neither had part in the creation, nor redemption of the
world, too many keepe no Sabbath, or at the most but a shadow
of a Sabbath. Where almost can wee finde one that will lose a
good bargaine rather than make it on the Lords day? Or that
will bridle his owne desires to sanctifie that day?

Seeing therefore this danger, in which thou maist easily bee
entrapped by the Deuils subtilty, and following the multitude; I
cannot but with all my power exhort thee, carefully to keepe
the Sabbath, to which end I pray thee marke well the fourth
Commaundement, *Remember that thou keepe holy the Sabbath day, six dayes shalt thou labour, and doe all that thou
hast to doe, but the seuenth is the Sabbath of the Lord thy
God, in it thou shalt doe no manner of worke, thou, nor thy
sonne, nor thy daughter, thy man seruant, nor thy maid-ser-
uant, nor thy cattle that is within thy gates: For in six dayes
the Lord made Heauen and Earth, the Sea, and all that is
therein, and rested the seuenth day, wherefore the Lord blessed
the seuenth day and hallowed it.*[1]

If thou wilt bee won to the due obseruation of this day as an
obedient seruant, see God commands, *Remember that thou
keepe holy the Sabbath day*. If as a louing and dutifull sonne,
see how GOD perswades thee, by equity, grounded vpon his
owne bounty to thee: Hee hath giuen thee six dayes to doe
thine owne workes, and hee requires but one of thee. What
canst thou say for thy selfe, why thou shouldest not wholly
that day giue thy selfe to his seruice? Lastly, if thou wilt

---

1 Exodus 20.8–11

learn how to serue him as a good scholar: hee teaches thee an< >
admirable way bothe by rule and example[,] first by rule thou
shalt do noe maner of worke in it, then by example. he made
the whole world in 6 days and he rested ye seuenthe whear-
630   fore he blessed it: &: seeinge god thus comands thee by his
power[,] perswades thee in his mercy and teaches thee bothe
by <y>rule and his own most gracious example: how canst
thou bee so deuoyd of grace as not to obey so iust a master[,]
so mercifull a father[,] so gracious a teacher; if thou make not
635   a consciens of keepinge this day howsoeuer a dull security
may possess thee to flatter thy selfe, thou indeed makest conscience of nothinge[.] for I am {perswaded} if thou canst dispence wth thy selfe to prophane this day; <thou wilt not>
eyther for thy profit or pleasure thou wilt not stick vppon the
640   like occasion to break all the rest of the comandement^s^ one
after another, thearfore for christs sake be watchefull that the
diuell deceyue you not nor non of his ministers draw thee
away from this days duty[.] he is allways busy and ready at
hand to draw thee from god but this day w^thout doupt he dou-
645   bles all his forces[,] he will provoke thine eys to sleep[,] he will
send heauines and dullnes to thy hart and perhaps payn to thy
body if hee can so much prevayle[.] any slight[,] any trick to
stay thee from gods house and from the congregatyon of his
people he will surely vse: nay hee will somtime do it wth reli-
650   gious pretenses as to pray at home[,] read a sermon[,] study the
scripture and to spend the time in such christian exercises as
are infinitly good at other times[.] but I once heard a religious
preacher affirm (and I beleeued him) that those whoo had abi-
lyt<ie>y of body to go to churche and yet out of any euill dis-
655   position (for good it cannot bee) absented themselues though
they prayd they wear not heard, it behooues the by how much
greater his practises are agaynst thee that day so much the
more to fortefy thy selfe agaynst him[.] at no hand let him stay
thee from the churche[,] thear god hathe promised to be
660   present, and thear he is. darest thou

---

630 &:] om.   **631** perswades thee] perswades   **633** grace] nay of Reason   **634** if] It
642 ministers] Instruments   **644** thee] thee away   **655** cannot] can hardly   **658** let
him] let them

645 learne how to serue him as a good Scholler, he teaches thee an
admirable way, both by rule and example. First, by rule, Thou
shalt doe no manner of worke in it: then by example, He made
the whole world in six dayes, and hee rested the seuenth,
wherefore hee blessed it.

650 Seeing God thus commands thee by his power, perswades
thee in his mercy, and teaches thee both by rule, and his owne
most gratious example, how canst thou bee so deuoid of grace,
nay of reason, as not to obey so iust a Master? so mercifull a
Father? so gracious a Teacher? If thou make not a conscience of[1]

655 keeping this day, howsoeuer a dull security may possesse thee
to flatter thy selfe, thou indeed makest conscience of nothing.
For I am perswaded, if thou canst dispence with thy selfe to
prophane this day, either for thy profit or pleasure, thou wilt
not sticke vpon[2] the like occasion to breake all the rest of the

660 Commandements one after another.
Therefore for Christs sake bee watchfull that the Deuill
deceiue you not, nor none of his instruments[3] draw thee away
from this dayes duty. Hee is alwaies busie and ready at hand to
draw thee away from God, but this day without doubt hee dou-

665 bles all his forces, hee will prouoke thine eies to sleepe, hee will
send heauinesse and dulnesse to thy heart, and perhaps paine to
thy body, if he can so much preuaile: any sleight, any tricke to
stay thee from Gods house, and from the Congregation of his
people, hee will surely vse, nay hee will sometimes doe it with

670 religious pretences, as to pray at home, reade a Sermon, study
the Scripture, and to spend the time in such Christian exercises,
as are infinitely good at other times. But I once heard a religious
Preacher affirme (and I beleeued him) that those who had ability of body to goe to Church, and yet out of any euill disposition

675 (for good it can hardly bee) absented themselues, though they
prayed, they were not heard.
It behoues thee by how much greater his practises are against
thee that day, so much the more to fortifie thy selfe against
him: at no hand[4] let him stay thee from the Church, there GOD

680 hath promised to bee present, and there hee is. Darest thou

---

1 make not a conscience of: make it not a matter of conscience
2 sticke vpon: hestitate
3 instruments: agents
4 at no hand: by no means

then silly wretch absent thy selfe from him? I know thou darest
not. go then wth a hart prepared to pray, by prayr, and goinge
meditate on gods great mercys in the creatyon of the world[,]
his greater mercy in redeeminge it and mingle wth thy
665   meditatyon prayrs that may apply theas great blessings to thy
selfe: so approche wth reuerent and feruent zeale the house of
god an[d] throwinge away all thoughts but such as may further
the good worke thou art about bend thy knees and hart to god
desiringe of him his holy spirit that thou maiest ioyn wth the
670   congregatyon in zealous prayr and earnest attentyon of his word
preached[.] and though thou hearest a minister preache as thou
thinkest weakly yet giue him thine attention and spend not the
time in readinge or any other meditations, and thou shalt finde
that he will deliuer somthinge profitable to thy soule eyther
675   that thou hast not heard before or not marked or forgotten and
it is fit thou shouldest bee often put in mind of those things
concern[ing] thy saluatyon[.] thus if thou spend thy time at
church thou wilt be ready to giue thy selfe to meditate of the
holy word thou hast heard w^thout wch truly hearinge profitethe
680   littlle[,] for it is wth the soule as wth the body though meat be
neuer so wholesom and the appetite neuer so great yet if any ill
disposition in the stomacke hinder digestion it turns not to
nourishment but rather proues more dangerous[,] so the word if
after hearinge it be not digested by meditatyon it is not nourish-
685   ing to ye soule[.] therefore let the time thou hast to bee absent
from churche be spent in praysinge god[,] prayinge to god and
applyinge to thy selfe what thou hast heard[.] if thou hast heard
a sin reprooued that thou art guilty of take it for a warninge[,]
do it no more[.] if thou hearest of a good action wch thou hast
690   ouerslipt striue to recouer time and resolue to put it in act[.]
thus by practising what thou hearest thou shalt binde it to thy
memory: and make thy selfe most happy: Learn of Isayah the
tru obseruatyon of the Sabathe: If thou turn away thy foot from
th<y>e sabathe from dooinge thy will on my holy day and call
695   the Sabathe a delighte to consecrate it as

---

666 approche] approach and Enter   670 of] to   671 though] though perhaps   672–3
and spend not the time in readinge or any other meditations,] *om.*   675 forgotten]
forgotten or not well put In practise   677 concern[ing]] concerning   692 and] and by
Making It thine owne

then, silly wretch, absent thy selfe from him? I know, thou darest not. Goe then with a heart prepared to pray by prayer, and
going meditate on Gods great mercies in the creation of the
world, his greater mercy in redeeming it, and mingle with thy
685   meditation prayers, that may apply these great blessings to thy
selfe.

    So approach and enter, with reuerent and feruent zeale, the
house of GOD, and throwing away all thoughts, but such as
may further the good worke thou art about, bend thy knees and
690   heart to God, desiring of him his holy Spirit, that thou maist
ioine with the Congregation in zealous prayer, and earnest
attention to his word preached. And though perhaps thou hearest a Minister preach, as thou thinkest, weakly, yet giue him
thine attention, and thou shalt finde that hee will deliuer some-
695   thing profitable to thy soule, either that thou hast not heard
before, or not marked, or forgotten, or not well put in practise.
And it is fit thou shouldest bee often put in minde of those
things concerning thy saluation.

    Thus if thou spend thy time at Church, thou wilt bee ready to
700   giue thy selfe to meditate of the holy Word thou hast heard,
without which truly hearing profiteth little. For it is with the
soule as with the body, though meat bee neuer so wholsome,
and the appetite neuer so great, yet if any ill disposition in the
stomacke hinder digestion, it turnes not to nourishment, but
705   rather proues more dangerous. So the Word if after hearing it
bee not digested by meditation, it is not nourishing to the soule.
Therefore let the time thou hast to bee absent from Church, bee
spent in praising God, praying to God, and applying to thy selfe
what thou hast heard. If thou hast heard a sinne reproued that
710   thou art guilty of, take it for a warning, doe it no more. If thou
hearest of a good action which thou hast ouerslipt,[1] striue to
recouer time, and resolue to put it in act. Thus by practising
what thou hearest, thou shalt binde it to thy memory, and by
making it thine owne, make thy selfe most happy.

715   Learne of *Isaiah*, the true obseruation of the Sabbath: If thou
turne away thy foot from the Sabbath, from doing thy will on
my holy day, and call the Sabbath a delight to consecrate it as

---

1 overslipt: passed over

gloryous [t]o the Lord, and shallt honor him not dooinge thy
own ways nor seekinge thine own will nor speaking a vayn
word. Then shallt thou delight in the Lord and I will caus thee
to mount vppon the high places of the earthe and feed the w^th
700   the heritage of Iacob thy father for the mouthe of the L hathe
spoken it. Isaiah. 58. 13. it is a wonder to see how often god
hathe comanded this one comandement and yet how slack wee
are to keep it[,] Exo: 31 from ye 12 verse is all comandinge this[,]
agayn in the 34 21 and < > ^diuers^ places more, learn then to
705   prepare thy hart early for this day wch if thou obseruest well god
will blesse the and thy Labors all the week: Thus far I k[h]aue
endeuored to exhort thee to thy duty towards god:[

]^12^[

] of wch the honor due to thy Parents is such a part as cannot bee
seperated for god comands it[:] Honor thy father and thy
710   mother[.] it is ye first comandement of the second table as, Thou
shall haue [n]oe other gods but me[,] is of ye first. Idolatry beeinge ye greatest sin agaynst god and disobedience to Parents
agaynst man wee are first warned of them as if wee should fall
into them it wear to late to auoyd the other; for if wee once
715   becom Idolaters it will be no hard matter to bee a bower down to
an image, to abuse gods holy name and to prophane his sab-
bathes: so if wee dare disobey good parents theft[,] murder[,]
adulltery[,] falsnes[,] couetousnes are easyly found out[,] nay I
dare say if thou breakest eyther of theas comandements thou
720   breakest all of the first and second table: for as thou canst not
bee idolatrous w^thout breakinge all the rest so thou canst not be
a disobedient childe but thou art <first> a murderer[,] a double
one[,] first of nature in thy selfe wch if thy wicked purposes do
not smother will of her selfe breake forthe into that duty, for an
725   example the story of Æneas shows how

---

706 k[h]aue] haue   707 god:] god of   711 shall] *om.*   711 [n]oe other] none others
712 Parents] parents being the ring lender In sinnes   713 if] If In case   715 becom]
be come In heart   716–17 sabbathes] sabbath   717 parents] parents at that
breach   718 are easyly found out] Easily Enter

glorious to the Lord, and shalt honour him, not doing thy owne
wayes, nor seeking thine owne will, nor speaking a vaine word:
720   Then shalt thou delight in the Lord, and I will cause thee to
mount vpon the high places of the earth, and feed thee with the
heritage of *Iacob* thy father, for the mouth of the Lord hath spoken it, *Isaiah* 58. 13.

It is a wonder to see how often God hath commanded this
725   one Commandement, and yet how slacke we are to keepe it.
Exod. 31. from the 12. verse, is all commanding this: againe in
the 34. 21. and diuers places more.

Learne then to prepare thy heart early for this day, which if
thou obseruest well, God will blesse thee and thy labours all
730   the weeke. Thus farre I haue endeuoured to exhort thee to thy
duty towards God.

12

Of which the honour due to thy Parents is such a part as cannot bee separated; for God commands it, *Honour thy father and
thy mother*, it is the first Commandement of the second table,
735   as, *Thou shal haue none other Gods but mee*, is of the first[1]:
Idolatry being the greatest sin against God, and disobedience to
parents, being the ring-leader in sinnes against man, wee are
first warned of them, as if in case we should fall into them, it
were too late to auoid the other. For if wee once become in
740   heart Idolaters, it will be no hard matter to be a bower down to
an Image, to abuse Gods holy Name, and to prophane his Sabbath: So if wee dare disobey good Parents, at that breach, theft,
murther, adultery, falsenesse, couetousnesse easily enter.

Nay, I dare say, if thou breakest either of these Commande-
745   ments, thou breakest all of the first and second Table: for as
thou canst not bee idolatrous without breaking all the rest, so
thou canst not bee a disobedient childe, but thou art a murderer, a double one: first of nature in thy selfe, which if thy
wicked purposes doe not smother, will of her selfe breake forth
750   into that duty. For an example, the story of *Aeneas* shewes how

---

1 Exodus 20.3, 12

much it was obserued by them that receyved not the comandement from gods own mouthe as did the Iews yet hee exposed
himselfe to all dangers rather then hee would forsake his father.
secondly thou art a murtherer of thy father whoo hauinge
730   stored vp all his ioy in thee hathe by thy disobedience; his gray
head brought wth sorrow to ye graue wch god forbid; and what
difference shall I say thear is between a disobedient childe and
an adullterer[?] the one forsakes the wife of his bosom[,] the
other forsakes the holy spirit[,] the sweet guide of his soule[.]
735   truly this is a fearfull adulltery and sin is a crafty strumpet[,]
she will allure thee and delude thee, agayn; in beeing disobedient thou art a theef[,] an impudent one[,] for thou doest not only
secretly steale but openly detayn the honor[,] reuerence and
obedient duty wch all the world can witnes is ^thy^ fathers and
740   how willt thou auoyd beeinge a fals witnes[?] will not one sin
draw on another[,] willt not thou bee ready to excuse thy selfe
by throwinge calumnious aspertyons on thy parents giuinge thy
tong leaue to ly agaynst thy conscience. and lastly (Oh Horrible[)] how easy a step is it to couet what thou thinkest thy par-
745   ents life <parents life> too long detayns from thee[?] thus thou
seest in beeinge disobedient thou breakest 6 comandements
from [which] I beseech allmighty god deliuer thee and giue thee
grace to bee obedient to him and to thy parents[.] I am sure thou
hast a father whoo will neuer comand thee any thing contrary
750   to the comandements of god[,] thearfore I haue no need to speak
to thee how far a father ought to bee obeyed but humbly desire
of god to continew him in his good desire wth long life[,] to
bringe thee vp in the fear of the L: and to giue thee a hart ready
to embrace all religious learning[.]

13

755   The next duty equall to this thou must perform to all the world
in generall[:] doo to all men as thou wouldst they should

---

729 murtherer] murther   732 thear is] Is theire   733–4 the wife ... his soule] hee had
his owne be^in^g   737 one] theefe   741 selfe] vnnaturall obstinacy   747 from] from
which outrage   747 deliuer] preserue   752 desire] desires   752 to] that he May

much it was obserued by them that receiued not the Commandement from Gods owne mouth, as did the Iewes, yet he
exposed himselfe to all dangers rather than hee would forsake
his father.[1] Secondly, thou art a murtherer of thy father, who
755 hauing stored vp all his ioy in thee, hath by thy disobedience
his gray head brought with sorrow to the graue; which God forbid.

And what difference, shall I say, is there betweene a disobedient childe, and an adulterer? the one forsakes her, by whom he
760 giueth being vnto others; the other despiseth those from whom
hee had his owne being. Truly this is a fearefull adultery, and
sinne is a crafty strumpet, she will allure thee and delude thee.

Againe, in being disobedient thou art a theefe, an impudent
theefe, for thou doest not onely secretly steale, but openly
765 detaine the honour, reuerence and obedient duty, which all the
world can witnesse is thy fathers.

And how wilt thou auoid being a false witnesse? will not one
sinne draw on another? Wilt not thou bee ready to excuse thy
vnaturall obstinacy, by throwing calumnious aspersions on thy
770 parents, giuing thy tongue leaue to lie against thy conscience?

And lastly (Oh horrible) how easie a step is it to couet what
thou thinkest thy parents life too long detaines from thee?

Thus thou seest in being disobedient thou breakest six Commandements, from which outrage, I beseech Almighty GOD
775 preserue thee, and giue thee grace to bee obedient to him, and to
thy parents. I am sure thou hast a father, who will neuer command thee any thing contrary to the Commandements of God.
Therefore I haue no need to speake to thee, how farre a father
ought to bee obeyed: but humbly desire of God to continue him
780 in his good desires with long life, that he may bring thee vp in
the feare of the Lord, and to giue thee a heart ready to embrace
all religious learning.

13

The next duty equall to this, thou must performe to all the
world in generall, Doe to all men as thou wouldst they should

---

1 The story of Aeneas saving his father, Anchises, from the burning of Troy occurs
in *The Aeneid*, Book 2.

doo vnto thee. this is the comandement our sauiour giues vs:
loue one another[,] by this wee shall bee known to bee his if
wee loue one another as hee hathe loued vs:

760   Yet of all that is comanded vs thear is nothinge more contrary to our wicked nature [than] this louinge our neyghbor as
our selfe[.] wee can wth eas enuy him if he be riche< > or scorn
him if hee be poor, but loue him? nay ye diuell hathe more craft
then so[,] it wear hard for him if men should once begin to loue

765   one another[,] thearfore hee [employs] all art to stir dissentyon
among as many as hee can and to mixe loue wth dissimu-
latyon[.] to auoyd this consider well that god is the author of
peace and loue, and that strifes and contentyons proceed of y^e
diuell, then if thou beest the childe of god doo the works of

770   god[,] loue thy neyghbor as he hathe comanded least thou
prouoke our blessed sauior (when he shall see that marke of the
diuell; malice in thee) to say as once to the vnbeleeuinge Iews[,]
you are of your father the diuell and the lusts of your father will
you doo Ioh: 8 44. Oh take heed thou offend not god thus greeu-

775   ously y^t hee shall disclaym thee as non of his because thou
doest not loue those that are his[,] this if well weyghed weare
enough to make euery man charitable if it wear only for fear to
hate whom god loued and to beleeue or iudge that god should
hate whear thou doest <whe> wear such an impious [v]ncharita-

780   blenes as a good christian must needs tremble at[.] god hathe
giuen thee no authoryty to iudge any man but he hathe comanded thee to loue thine enemy, loue your enemis[,] <to> blesse
them that curs you[,] doo good to them that hate you and pray
for them that hurt ^&^ persecute you that you may bee the

785   children of your father wch is in heauen Math: 5 44, A man may
finde ways enough to possess the diuell of his soule but non w^th
lesse plesure to himselfe then this; he may sell it as did Iudas to
satisfy a couetous desire. he may loose it as does many a lazy
man his worldly estate because he will not troble himselfe <he

790   sinks> to look ouer an account of his fortune[,] he sinks ear he
thinks of it[,] so fares it wth a

---

761 nature] nature then   762 selfe] selfes   765 hee] hee vseth   773 lusts] lust   778
and] but

785   doe vnto thee. This is the commandement our Sauiour giues vs;
      Loue one another: by this wee shall bee knowne to be his, if we
      loue one another, as hee hath loued vs.[1]
          Yet of all that is commanded vs, there is nothing more con-
      trary to our wicked nature than this louing our neighbour as our
790   selues. Wee can with ease enuie him if hee be rich, or scorne
      him if he be poore; but loue him? nay the Deuill hath more
      craft than so. It were hard for him if men should once begin to
      loue one another: therefore hee vseth all Art to stir dissention
      among as many as he can, & to mix loue with dissimulation.
795   To auoid this, consider well that God is the Author of peace
      and loue, and that strifes and contentions proceed of the Deuill.
      Then if thou beest the child of God, doe the workes of God,
      loue thy neighbour as he hath com[m]anded, lest thou prouoke
      our blessed Sauiour, when hee shall see, that marke of the
800   Deuill, malice in thee, to say as once to the vnbeleeuing Iewes,
      You are of your father the deuill, and the lusts of your father
      will you doe, *Ioh*. 8. 44.
          Oh take heed thou offend not God thus grieuously, that hee
      shall disclaime thee as none of his, because thou doest not loue
805   those that are his.
          This, if well weighed, were enough to make euery man chari-
      table, if it were onely for feare to hate whom God loued. But to
      beleeue or iudge that God should hate where thou doest, were
      such an impious vncharitablenesse as a good Christian must
810   needs tremble at. God hath giuen thee no authoritie to iudge
      any man, but he hath commanded thee to loue thine enemie;
      Loue your enemies, blesse them that curse you, doe good to
      them that hate you, and pray for them that hurt and persecute
      you, that you may be the children of your father which is in
815   heauen, *Matth*. 5. 44.
          A man may finde wayes enow to possesse the Deuill of his
      soule, but none with lesse pleasure to himselfe than this: hee
      may sell it, as did *Iudas*, to satisfie a couetous desire;[2] hee may
      lose it, as does many a lazie man his worldly estate; because hee
820   will not trouble himselfe to looke ouer an account of his for-
      tune, hee sinkes ere hee thinkes of it; so fares it with a

---

1 John 13.34–5
2 Matthew 26.14–16

negligent christian, 3dly he may pawn it like a foolish vnthrift
whoo pawns that wch should keep him all his life to< > purchase
a gay toy wch shall serue him a day or too[,] so dothe hee y^t

795   pawns that rich Iewell his soule <his soule> to ye couetous
diuell for plesure[,] happely he [m]eans to redeem it but runs on
his selfe pleasing cours till the vse hathe deuoured the principall and his vnmercifull creditor hales him to a du[n]geon whear
he has time foreuer to bewayle not only his present misery but

800   the loss of infinit happines:
      Theas are strange enough, that ^a man^ should sell eternyty
of ioy for welthe, or sleep away the time whearin he might
make such a purchase, or pawn an inestimable tresure for
things not worthe esteem. but yet they are all better then hee

805   that giues his soule for nothinge as dothe the enuious man. the
couetous gets riches[,] the slothefull eas, the wanton pleasure
but this hater of his brother gets nothinge but torment[,] fret-
tinge and vexatyon: he is not the fatter for his meat nor dothe
hee rest though hee sleep[,] yet he for whom he thus toyls his

810   spirits happely eats[,] sleeps and laughs at his folly or peradventure pittys him. the more easily to auoyd this sin consider well
the <profit and> disprofits of it[,] <the disprofits> read in the
first: epist[le] of St Iohn 3 chap 14 and 15 verses and in the 4th ch
the 8 and the 20 verses, read the 13 of the first to the corinths[,]

815   thear St Paul shows that all vertues are of no force wthout this
loue. as the want of it brings infinit misery so the possession
infinit Ioy[.] first wee perform christs comandement whoo often
requires this of vs as if he should say[,] I haue satisfyed my
father for all the comandemen^ts^ that you haue broke[,] now

820   your taske is easy[,] I leaue you nothinge to doo but to loue one
another[,] do this and you doo all: you fullfill the law Ro the 13
the 8 and 10 verses[,] you abide in the light the i Ep of St Iohn 2:
10[.]

---

795 couetous] griping vsurer the   796 [m]eans] meanes one day   805 giues] giues
away   807 this] the   807 nothinge] nothing no not In present   809 whom]
^w^hom<> or against whom   810 spirits] spirit   810 his] his enuier^s^   814 the 8]
8   815–16 all vertues ... this loue] with out Charitie Euen spirituall graces are of no
worth   817 first] by Charitie   817 christs] our Sauiour Christ   821 all: you] all by It
we   822 you] by It wee   822 the i Ep of S^t] i

negligent Christian. Thirdly, hee may pawne it, like a foolish
vnthrift, who pawnes that which should keepe him all his life,
to purchase a gay toy, which shall serue him a day or two: so
825   doth hee that pawnes that rich iewell his soule, to the griping[1]
vsurer the Deuill, for pleasure; haply hee meanes one day to
redeeme it, but runnes on his selfe-pleasing course till the vse
hath deuoured the principall,[2] and his vnmercifull Creditor
hales[3] him to a dungeon, where he has time for euer to bewaile,
830   not only his present misery, but the losse of infinite happinesse.

These are strange enough that a man should sell eternitie of
ioy for wealth, or sleepe away the time wherein hee might
make such a purchase, or pawne an inestimable treasure for
things not worth esteeme. But yet they are all better than hee
835   that giues away his soule for nothing, as doth the enuious man.
The couetous gets riches, the slothfull ease, the wanton pleasure, but this hater of his brother gets nothing (no not in present)
but torment, fretting and vexation: he is not the fatter for his
meat, nor doth hee rest though hee sleepe, yet he for whom, or
840   against whom hee thus toiles his spirit, haply eats, sleepes, and
laughes at his enuiers folly, or peraduenture pitties him.

The more easily to auoid this sinne, consider well the disprofits of it. Reade in the first Epistle of Saint *Iohn* 3. Chap. 14. and
15. Verses, and in the 4. chap. the 8. and the 20. verses: reade
845   the 13. of the first to the *Corinthians*; there Saint *Paul* shewes
that without charitie euen spirituall graces are of no worth. As
the want of it brings infinite miserie, so the possession infinite
ioy. By Charitie wee performe our Sauiour Christs commandement, who often requires this of vs, as if hee should say, I haue
850   satisfied my father for all the commandements that you haue
broke. Now your taske is easie, I leaue you nothing to doe, but
to loue one another; doe this and you doe all. By it we fulfill the
Law, *Rom* 13. 8. and 10. verses. By it wee abide in the light, I
Ioh. 2. 10.

---

1 griping: grasping
2 the vse hath deuoured the principall: the interest owed has surpassed the value of
   the capital
3 hales: hauls

825 is it possible when theas are well weyghed that any man should
bee so mad to bear an vncharitable hart about him or so foole
hardy to harbor a spleen that shall hasard his saluatyon[?] can
wee be so cruell to our selues as to deny christ one comandement[?] for all his loue to vs he requires but this testimony of
our loue to him wch wee cannot chuse but perform if wee doo
830 loue him[,] thearfore take heed if thou feel any malice toward
thy brother[,] be sure thy hart is not vpright toward god[,] thearfore so root it from thy hart that no string of it be left for it will
grow faster then Ionahs gourd:

Answear me not wth flesh and bloud cannot doo this. I know
835 it but if thou desire god to giue thee his holy spirrit thou shallt
be strong to suffer and ready to forgiue[,] thou must not in any
thing be subiect to the fleshe for the wisdom of the flesh is
deathe but allways make the spirrit thy guide for thear is life
and peace[.] the diuell would desire no greater advantage then
840 that thou wouldest trust thy soule to the discretyon of thy corrupt fleshe[,] he would soon force that to betray thee[,] but when
thou hast put thy selfe vnder the spirrit submittinge thy will to
the will of god he is no more able to hurt thee.

The next excuse I would take from thee is a very foolish one
845 but so comon that I fear you may happen on it and that is this[:]
if I should suffer wrongs patiently what will becom of my reputation[,] what will the world say: truly if you remember christ
hathe suffered more for you then it is possible for you to suffer
yet he neuer reviled any of his enemis nor strake his persecu-
850 tors but prayed for them and by his example teaches all that
loue him to do the like[,] he wills you to turn [t]he left cheek to
him that smote the right[,] to giue to him that takes from you
and to go wth him that compells you: but theas are strange rules
for a generous spirit in theas times[.] nay sure if I bee struck I
855 must strike agayn els I am a coward, indeed for giuinge if it
wear to one that would desire

829–30 wch wee ... loue him] <u>om</u>.   831–2 thearfore] <u>om</u>.   832 it] It out   832 string]
sting   833 gourd] ground   834 cannot doo] canno   841 force] Inueigle   850 by]
<u>om</u>.   855 indeed] Indeed as

855   Is it possible, when these are well weighed, that any man
should bee so mad to beare an vncharitable heart about him, or
so foole hardy to harbour a spleene[1] that shall hazard his saluation? Can wee be so cruell to our selues, as to deny Christ one
commandement? For all his loue to vs, he requires but this tes-
860   timony of our loue to him, which we cannot choose but performe if we doe loue him. Therefore take heed if thou feele any
malice towards thy brother, bee sure thy heart is not vpright[2]
toward God. So root it out from thy heart, that no sting of it bee
left, for it will grow faster than *Ionahs* Gourd.[3]

865   Answer mee not with Flesh and bloud cannot doe this: I
know it. But if thou desire God to giue thee his holy Spirit, thou
shalt bee strong to suffer, and ready to forgiue. Thou must not
in any thing bee subiect to the flesh, for the wisdome of the
flesh is death. But alwayes make thy spirit thy guide, for there
870   is life and peace.

The deuill would desire no greater aduantage than that thou
wouldst trust thy soule to the discretion of thy corrupt flesh, he
would soone inueigle[4] that to betray thee. But when thou hast
put thy selfe vnder the spirit, submitting thy will to the will of
875   God, he is no more able to hurt thee.

The next excuse I would take from thee, is a very foolish one,
but so common, that I feare you may happen on it, and that is
this; If I should suffer wrongs patiently, what will become of my
reputation? what will the world say? Truly if you remember,
880   Christ hath suffred more for you, than it is possible for you to
suffer: yet hee neuer reuiled any of his enemies, nor strake his
persecutors, but prayed for them. And his example teaches all
that loue him to doe the like. He wils you to turne the left
cheeke to him that smote the right, to giue to him that takes
885   from you, and to goe with him that compels you.[5]

But these are strange rules for a generous spirit in these
times, nay sure if I be strucke I must strike againe, else I am a
coward. Indeed as for giuing, if it were to one that would desire

---

1 spleene: grudge
2 vpright: unbending
3 *Ionahs* Gourd: Jonah 4.6
4 inueigle: beguile
5 Matthew 5.39–42

it at my hands I had rather giue a fragment of my right then go
to law but if he will not sue to me Ile spend all I am worthe eare
I yeeld, or I would go out of m[y] door to show a man his way
860   but I would fayn see whoo could compell mee[.] I marry[,] this is
of the right streyn[,] but now look wth a considerate ey vppon
this custom of the wor[ld] and the former comandement of
christ and thou shallt finde the[m] iust oposit[.] thearfore take
heed and let it bee thy cheef care neuer to prise thy reputation
865   wth men equall to the salluation of thyne own soule but if thou
desirest to keep thy credit vnblemishe^d^ serue god wth an
vpright hart and doo nothinge to any man y^t thou wouldst not
bee content hee should doo vnto thee[.] open thy hand to the
poor according to thy ability[,] meddle not wth othe[r] mens
870   occasions but whear [thou] maies[t] doo good and if it bee in thy
powr to hurt thine enemy let it pass[,] doo him good if thou
canst and boast not of it[,] he that sees the in priuat will openly
reward thee[.] lastly let thy hart be kept allways in aw of this
want of charyty by continuall remembringe that thou hast noe
875   form of prayr to desire forgiue< >nes for thy selfe if thou forgiue
not others[,] all other petitions god grants vs freely[,] only this is
conditionall[:] he forgiue vs as wee forgiue others[,] our sauior
hathe taught vs no other way to desire it and in the 18 of
Mathew he shows god will no otherwise grant it[.]

---

869 othe[r]] om.   870 occasions] occasion   870 whear] whe^r^e thou   870 and] and
hast a Calling to it and   874 hast noe] hast of thy sauiour no other   875–6 if thou
forgiue not] than that wherin thou Couenantest to forgiue   876 all] all the   876
petitions god grants vs freely] petitions wee present vnto god absolutely

890 it at my hands, I had rather giue a fragment of my right than goe to law, but if hee will not sue to mee, Ile spend all I am worth ere I yeeld: Or I would goe out of my doore to shew a man his way, but I would faine see who could compell mee. I mary,[1] this is of the right straine; but now looke with a consid-
895 erate eye vpon this custome of the world, and the former Commandement of Christ, and thou shalt finde them iust opposite.

Therefore take heed, and let it bee thy chiefe care neuer to prize thy reputation with men equall to the saluation of thine owne soule. But if thou desirest to keepe thy credit vnblemished, serue God with an vpright heart, and doe nothing to any
900 man, that thou wouldest not bee content hee should doe vnto thee. Open thy hand to the poore according to thy abilitie, meddle not with other mens occasions,[2] but where thou maist doe good, and hast a calling to it. And if it bee in thy power to hurt thine enemy, let it passe, doe him good if thou canst, and boast
905 not of it: he that sees thee in priuate, will openly reward thee.

Lastly, let thy heart bee kept alwayes in awe of this want of charity, by continuall remembring that thou hast of thy Sauiour no other forme of praier to desire forgiuenesse for thy selfe, than that wherein thou couenantest to forgiue others. All the other
910 petitions wee present vnto God absolutely: onely this is conditionall, hee forgiue vs as wee forgiue others. Our Sauiour hath taught vs no other way to desire it, and in the 18. of *Matthew* hee shewes God will no otherwise grant it.

Sine fine finis.[3]

---

1 I mary: indeed (an expression of indignation)
2 occasions: affairs
3 *Sine fine finis*: end without end

Textual Variants

Variants are listed by the page and line numbers of the second impression as it appears in this edition. Each emandation is followed by its source(s). The spelling of the variant derives from its earliest source.

Goad: *The Mothers Legacie to her vnborne Childe*. British Library, Additional MS 4378.

   A: *The Mothers Legacie, To her vnborne Childe*. Iohn Hauiland for William Barret. London, 1624.

   B: *The Mothers Legacie, To her vnborne Childe*. 3rd Imp. Iohn Hauiland for Hanna Barret. London, 1625.

   C: *The Mothers Legacie, To her vnborne Childe*. 6th Imp. E. A. for Robert Allot. London, 1632.

   D: *The Mothers Legacie, to her unborne Childe*. 7th Imp. F. K. for Robert Allot. London, 1635.

   E: *The Mothers Legacy To Her Unborn Child*. J. Wilmot. Oxford, 1684.

'The Approbation.'

41.16	*A Testament*] *omitted Goad*
41.16	Heb. 9. 17.] *omitted Goad, C, D;* Heb. 3. 17. *E*
42.30	heretofore] theretofore *Goad*
42.38	sometime] sometimes *Goad*
42.40	of] *omitted Goad*
42.41	carefully] carefull *Goad*

42.45	2 Tim. 3. 15, 16.] *omitted C, D, E*
43.53	blessing] blessings *Goad*
43.60–1	husband] husband (which the Printer is pleased to stile by the name of an Epistle Dedicatory) *A*
43.74	of] off *E*
43.80	or phrase] *omitted A*
43.84	reason] Reasons *Goad*
43.84	about] aboue *C, D*
43.87–44.90	which Treatise ... hereafter followeth.] *omitted A*
44.89–90	followeth] followed *Goad*
44.111	and] a *Goad*
45.126	practise] pra<yer>ctis *Goad*
45.127–8	*Sic approbauit/*Tho. Goad.] *omitted A*

'To my ... dearly loued Husband'

47.5	I so] so *Goad*
47.9	wanting me] want *Goad*
47.17	inclination] inclinations *E*
47.24	these] those *Goad*
49.26	vnderstood] vnderstand *C, D, E*
49.27	to a better] to better *A*
49.39	seuerely] seueraly *C*
49.42	her] *omitted Goad*
49.48–9	thought old] taught ould *Goad*
49.55	he] it *C, D, E*
49.55	of] *omitted C, D, E*
49.58	all] *omitted Goad*
51.68–9	Shee is- Indeed] she is indeed *Goad;* She is, Indeed *B;* She is indeed *C, D, E*
51.79	that] the contrary *E*
51.80	worthy] worthy of *E*
51.80	for] *omitted Goad*
51.89–90	knowes himself shall] *omitted Goad*
53.99	of] for *A*
53.100	seruants] seruant *Goad*
53.100	than] that *Goad*
53.106–7	There wants ... euery doore.] *omitted Goad, A, E*
53.112	the other] another *C, D, E*
53.118	to] vnto *C, D, E*

53.125	seuere] serue *C;* secure *D, E*
53.127	skilfully] skilfull *Goad*

The Mothers Legacie, To her vnborne Childe

59.31	The] *omitted A*
59.46	nor] not *Goad*
61.71	endeuour] endeavour to apply *E*

(1)

63.104	my first] and my *Goad*
63.106	will I] I will *C, D*
63.114	not breake thy promises] *omitted Goad*
63.116	marke] make *C, D*
63.116–17	thy life, ... will blesse] *omitted Goad*

(2)

63.122	thine owne weaknesse.] *omitted Goad*
65.133	thou once] thy heart *C, D*
65.133	but] *omitted Goad*
65.135	vnapt, and thy heart more] *omitted Goad*
65.144	than] that *C*
65.153–6	you, that ... to serue] *omitted Goad*
65.156	tentations] temptations *E*
65.163–4	humble thankes, that] *omitted Goad*

(3)

67.178	Oh] Oh, doe *C, D, E*
67.189	eye] eyes *C, D, E*

(4)

69.211	Be ashamed of idlenesse] *omitted Goad*
69.213	tentations] temptations *E*
69.227	created] createst *C, D, E*
69.230	good] God *Goad*

(5)

71.238	Is it] It is *Goad*
71.245	reason:] reason. How *E*
71.248	way.] way? *E*
71.255	wilt] shalt *Goad, B, C, D, E*
71.257–8	if not to out-goe them] *omitted Goad*
71.262	dresse] presse *C, D*
73.297	as] a *Goad*
73.299	women] woman *Goad*
75.307	that] than *C*
75.313	but if … take it,] *omitted Goad*
75.319	thee see] see *Goad*
75.322–3	tiptoes, reckning their] *omitted Goad*
75.325	it is] is it *C*
75.326	flatterer] flattery *A*
75.335	threatning] threatnings *C, E*
77.349	thy] the *E*
77.352	life] liue *Goad*

(6)

77.357–8	and vse … in any.] Use such Praiers as are publickly allowed, and chiefly those appointed by the Church. *E*
77.360	Prayer] Praier in your private Devotions *E*

(7)

79.372	creation] Recreation *Goad, A, B, C, D, E*
79.377	honor] *honor.* I Jo. 12. 26. *E*
79.383	I] *omitted Goad*
79.387	&c.] *omitted Goad*
79.390–1	learnest, the more thou wilt desire, and the more thou] *omitted Goad*

(8)

79.397	all] *omitted D*
79.397	thee] *omitted* Goad
83.446	23] 32 *C, D, E*
83.448	*preserue*] preferre *C, D, E*

(9)

85.493	&c.] *omitted Goad*
85.494–5	*And I ... with thee.*] *And there is none upon Earth I desire in comparison of thee. E*
85.507	his] this *A*
87.512	casts] cast *C*
87.522	these] those *Goad*
87.530	doe well] doe it *C, D;* still act *E*
87.539	to] *omitted E*
87.539–40	but it ... Rebuke not] *omitted Goad*
91.582	thou couldst resist all others] *omitted Goad*

(10)

91.606	Last] Lastly *C, D, E*
91.607	as] and *C, D*
91.607–9	Doctor *Smiths* ... mans prayer.] Some good Book of Praiers allowed by the Church, when thine own Meditations afford not sufficient matter for thy evening Devotions. *E*
91.612	Sabbath] Seventh *E*
91.613	*Remember*] *omitted Goad*

(11)

93.614	the Sabbath day. This] *omitted Goad*
93.616	confirmed] far extends it self *E*
93.616	in] under *E*
93.616–17	by the ... is called] that we are to keep Holy one Day in Seven, the first Day of the Week, in memory of our Saviors *Resurrection*, called therefore *E*
93.618	perpetually] perpetuall *Goad*
93.620	Sabbath] such time *E*
93.620–1	a shadow of a Sabbath] in appearance *E*
93.625	and] and by *E*
93.627	the Sabbath, to which] this Day without doing any servile *work* thereon unles Necessity, or Charity requires it. To this *E*
93.633	*gates*] Gate *C, D, E*
93.636	*it.*] *it. And as the Jews their Sabbath, so we ought to Sanctify the Lords Day. E*

93.638	*that*] omitted E
93.639	*the Sabbath day.*] &c E
93.640	GOD] god commands Remember that thou keepe holy the Sabbath day If as a louing and dutiefull Sonne see how god *Goad*
95.650–1	perswades thee] perwades *Goad*
95.657	For] omitted E
95.669	nay] and C, D, E
97.684	greater] great C, D, E
97.715	obseruation of the Sabbath] way of keeping a Day Holy to the Lord E
99.724	a] omitted C, D
99.724	hath] omitted E
99.725	and yet ... keepe it] to the *Jews* E
99.727	more.] more. And certainly *Christians* ought to be no les carefull in observing the *Lords* Day. E
99.731	God] god of *Goad*

(12)

99.735	*shal*] omitted *Goad*
99.737	ring-leader] ring lender *Goad*
99.747	a] a swearer, a D; a stubborn and E
101.759–60	her, by ... from whom] omitted *Goad*
101.774	which] which greivous E
101.780	desires] desire C, D

(13)

101.783	thou must] must thou E
103.792	him] him to prevail over so many E
103.793	Art] Arts E
103.801	lusts] lust *Goad*
105.837	this] the *Goad*, B, C, D, E
105.839–40	or against whom] omitted E
105.844	the] omitted *Goad*
105.848	Christs] Christ *Goad*
105.853–4	I *Ioh*] I *Epist Iohn* A
107.856	mad] mad as C, D, E

107.859	requires] reputes *C, D, E*
107.860–1	which we ... loue him] *omitted Goad*
107.864	Gourd] ground *Goad*
107.865	doe] *omitted Goad*
107.869	thy] the *A, B, D, E*
109.893	of] *omitted C, D, E*
109.902	occasions] occasion *Goad*
109.907	continuall] continually *D, E*
109.914	*Sine fine finis.*] *omitted Goad;* FINIS. *A*

Appendix:
Nineteenth-Century
Introductions to
The Mothers Legacy

1 ROBERT LEE (1852)

The / Mothers Legacie, / To her vnborne / Childe. / By Elizabeth / Ioceline. / Reprinted from the Edition of 1625. / With A / Biographical and Historical Introduction. / William Blackwood & Sons, / Edinburgh and London. / 1852.

To
The Most Honourable
The Lady Sophia Hastings,
Marchioness of Bute,
This Reprint
of
'The Mother's Legacie'
Is Most Respectfully
Inscribed.

MADAM, – About four years ago, soon after the birth of your son, a copy of the third edition of *The Mother's Legacie* was put into your hands; and the opinion expressed by your Ladyship, after an attentive perusal, induced the owner of the little volume to publish a facsimile impression of that early and genuine edition. The fulfilment of this purpose appeared to be only an act of justice to the author, as the Editor had seen, appended to a volume of modern sermons, published in

1840, what was represented to be 'a reprint' from an edition printed at the Theatre, Oxford, in 1684, 'for the satisfaction of the person of quality herein concerned.' But this reprint, however faithfully it may have copied an Oxford edition, is really a spurious impression, as it contains several unwarrantable deviations from the original text, – to an extent which, in several instances, materially alters the author's meaning. If the variations thus introduced were meant to be decided improvements, the grounds for adopting them should have been fairly and honestly avowed; but, before adverting farther to this particular, it may be proper to give some account of the author, and of the peculiar circumstances under which her mind was cultivated, and her religious character was formed.

Her name was Elizabeth Brooke, daughter of Sir Richard Brooke of Norton, whose first wife was the only daughter of William Chaderton, a native of Nuthurst, near Manchester, who was educated at Cambridge, where he became a Fellow of Christ's College, and was appointed Lady Margaret's Professor of Divinity in 1567, and Master of Queen's College in 1568, in which office he is said by Sir John Harrington to have been beloved by the scholars, because his authority was tempered with courtesy. In 1579 he was appointed Bishop of Chester, and in 1596 he was consecrated Bishop of Lincoln, where he died in 1608. In early life he was chaplain to Robert Dudley, Earl of Leicester, from whom, as well as from Lord Burghley, and many other noblemen and gentlemen of great influence and power, a number of letters to him have been inserted in the 3d and 4th books of Peck's *Desiderata Curiosa*, from some of which it appears that the Bishop was considered too indulgent towards the Puritans. Thus, on the 2d of May 1581, Edwin Sandys, the Archbishop of York, wrote to him privately, 'My Lord, you are noted to yield too much to general fastings, all the day preaching and praying. Verily a good exercise in time and upon just occasion, when it cometh from good authority. But (when there is none occasion, neither the thing commanded by the prince or a synod) the wisest and best learned cannot like of it, neither will her Majesty permit it. There lurketh matter under that pretended piety. The devil is crafty, and the young ministers of these our times grow mad.' How the Bishop acted, in consequence of this private advice, is not very clearly ascertained; but there is reason to believe that he was as lenient as he was wont to be in the exercise of his authority, and he was countenanced in his moderation by some of the most powerful of the nobles, including Lord Burghley, the Earls of Bedford, Warwick, and Leicester, and above all Henry, third Earl of Huntingdon, who that very year (Dec. 7, 1581) wrote a letter to this Bishop of Chester, strongly commending him for establishing lectureships and daily morning prayers at Manchester and other parishes, and who, in another letter the following year, (Dec. 12, 1582,) expressed his cordial approbation of the Bishop's exemplary zeal and kindness in encouraging all the good ministers who were under him.

About the year 1569, it is understood that Bishop Chaderton was married, and his only child, Jane, became afterwards the first wife of Sir Richard Brooke of Norton, son and heir of Thomas Brooke, sheriff of Chester, and Anne, daughter of Lord Audley. There is some reason to believe that the marriage of the Bishop's daughter proved not altogether happy. Sir John Harrington, in his account of the bishops, written about the year 1606, has said of Bishop Chaderton – 'He now remains at Lincoln, in very good estate, having only one daughter married to a knight of good worship, though now, they living asunder, he may be thought to have had no great comfort of that matrimony, yet to her daughter he means to leave a great patrimony.' There is no doubt that a serious misunderstanding had existed, which led to a permanent separation.

A more painful rumour has been preserved in Sir Ralph Winwood's *State Papers*, vol. iii. p. 385; but it is to be remembered that this work abounds more in hearsay tales and idle gossip than in authentic information. The story relates to a period when Jane Chaderton (Lady Brooke) had been dead several years, and when her daughter was a mere child; and yet one or the other is represented as having been betrayed into a fatal intimacy with at least one person of flagitious life. But the particulars of the narrative are self-contradictory, and could easily be demonstrated to be a malignant and baseless fabrication.[1]

From such slanderous allegations, proving that the materials of biography are often gathered from the most questionable sources, it is refreshing to turn to the unvarnished picture of domestic life exhibited in the scanty memorials of the granddaughter of Bishop Chaderton, furnished by Dr Thomas Goad, chaplain to Archbishop

---

1 The reviewer of the 1852 edition for *Gentleman's Magazine* argues that these rumours must have referred to Richard Brooke's second wife, rather than Jane Chaderton Brooke (497).

Abbot, who in this capacity possessed the power of licensing books.*
As the son of Dr Roger Goad, provost of King's College, Cambridge,
he had the best opportunities of knowing the family of Bishop Chaderton; and, according to his testimony, the Bishop – who survived his
own daughter several years – had bestowed the utmost pains to train
up his only grandchild in the most solid and serious, as well as the
most elegant, branches of learning in which, during the greater part
of the sixteenth century, no inconsiderable proportion of ladies of
rank in England attained high proficiency. Dr Goad's enumeration of
the female accomplishments in which she was nurtured includes
languages and other liberal arts; but, above all, that pious discipline
of the mind, which is both the beginning and the consummation of
the wisdom which is from above.

The range of this young lady's studies is not represented as sur-
passing what had been cultivated by females of the same station for
nearly a hundred years. Sir Thomas More – whose first child was a
daughter born about the year 1508, who died in 1544 – is generally
represented as the first who introduced a profound acquaintance
with the classics and other branches of polite literature as essential
constituents of a lady's education. This daughter, afterwards Mrs
Roper, wrote Latin with such taste and accuracy as to excite the
admiration of Erasmus and the incredulity of Cardinal Pole. Her
daughter's talents and erudition were scarcely inferior. The example
of Sir Thomas More was followed by Henry VIII. in the cases of the
Princesses Mary and Elizabeth. Mary translated part of the paraphrase of Erasmus on St John's Gospel, printed in 1548, and dedicated to Queen Catherine, by Nicholas Udall, who takes special
notice of 'the great number of noble women at that time in England,
not only given to the study of human sciences and strange tongues,
but also so thoroughly expert in the Holy Scriptures that they were
able to compare with the best writers, as well in enditing and pen-
ning of godly and fruitful treatises, as also in translating good books
out of Latin or Greek into English; and it was now a common thing
to see young virgins so trained in the study of good letters that they
willingly set all vain pastimes at nought for learning's sake.'

This Queen (Catherine Parr) had been herself educated in polite

---

* Of Dr Thomas Goad, Fuller, in his *Worthies of England,* says he was 'a great and
general scholar, exact critic, historian, poet, schoolman, divine. He was substi-
tuted by King James in the place of Dr Hall, and sent over to the synod of Dort.'

learning; and several of her works were printed – particularly *Prayers and Meditations* in 1545, and the *Lamentation of a Sinner* soon after her death in 1548, with a preface by Lord Burghley. Lord Burghley – who at this time was only twenty-eight years of age – had been twice married, and, in both cases, to ladies of extraordinary attainments in literature: first, in 1541, to Mary Cheke, sister of Sir John Cheke, Professor of Greek at Cambridge, and tutor to Edward VI.; secondly, in 1545, to Mildred Cooke, who is said by Roger Ascham to have been one of the two best Greek scholars of the ladies of his time – the other being Lady Jane Grey. Mildred was the first of the daughters of Sir Anthony Cooke, who, as well as Sir John Cheke, was one of the tutors of King Edward. His second daughter, Anne, was mother of Lord Bacon, and was eminent both for her piety and her correct acquaintance with the Greek, Latin, and Italian languages. She, and two younger sisters, Lady Russell and Lady Killigrew, published several works indicating great talents and attainments. Anne Cecil, the eldest daughter of Lord Burghley, afterwards Countess of Oxford, was also a lady of singular accomplishments. It would be very easy to add to this list many other names whose reputation for learning was understood to be tinctured with Puritanical tendencies.

It is natural to conceive that Chaderton, the friend of such men as Sir Anthony Cooke and Sir William Cecil, (Lord Burghley,) both of whom had been educated in Cambridge not long before he studied there, would follow their example in the training of his daughter and granddaughter, more especially as a similar practice had then become prevalent in families of rank. From Dr Goad's account, it is evident that the granddaughter was ardent and assiduous in her application to the study of poetry, history, and morality – availing herself of her intimacy with foreign tongues. At the age of twenty she was married, but of the family of her husband little appears to be known. Dr Fuller, in his *Worthies of Cheshire*, says that Bishop Chaderton's grandchild, a virtuous gentlewoman of rare accomplishments, married to *Mr Joceline, Esquire*, being big with child, wrote a book of advice, since printed, and entitled *The Mother's Legacie to her Unborn Infant*, of whom she died in travail. Betham, in his *Baronetage of England*, (vol. ii. p. 334, &c.,) says, 'that Sir Richard Brocke, by his first wife, Jane Chaderton, had one daughter, *Mary*, wife of Thorold Joseline, Esq. of Hogington, in Cambridgeshire, who had her mother's lands.' As Betham mistakes the Christian name of both the lady and the gentleman, his statement is not entitled to claim implicit credit; but it is a well ascertained fact that the manor of Hokington, or Oakington, about five miles from Cambridge, was, for some years after the Reformation, in the family of the Joscelyns, and afterwards became the property of Queen's College, Cambridge. It is probable that Tourell Joceline was a relation of Archbishop Parker's chaplain, John Joscelyn, who, according to Strype, was an Essex man, and sometimes wrote his name John Goscelin. The name was not uncommon in England, nor even in Scotland; for, in the *Ragman Roll*, we find, in 1296, William Goscelyn, del counte de Selkyrk; and the name Joscelyn, about the same period, existed also in the neighbouring county of Peebles. John Joscelyn is well known as a Saxon scholar, who gave great assistance to Archbishop Parker in his work *On the Antiquity of the British Church*, if, indeed, he did not write the entire book. But though the name of Tourell Joceline has not been registered either in the annals of learning, or in the history of his country, it is most satisfactory to know that he possessed the unbounded confidence and affection of his amiable wife, whose letter, addressed to him in the immediate prospect of death, is so tender and touching, and so replete with practical wisdom and hallowed principles, that no human being who is not past feeling can read it without deep emotion. Of the maternal counsels bequeathed to the unborn child, it is unnecessary to anticipate the judgment of the reader. We are told by Dr Goad, that 'this small treatise was found in her desk unfinished;' and it is affecting to know that the serenity of her mind, in looking forward to the eternal world, was not unclouded by occasional visitations of sadness; but these seasons of affliction were happily instrumental in weaning her from the deceitful allurements of things temporal, and establishing her soul in the perfect work of patience, and in the blessed hope of an eternal weight of glory.

It has already been noticed, that in at least one (and probably more than one) edition of this little work, several alterations have been inserted, without any explanation or apology ... Is it the part of an honest editor to assume the liberty of withdrawing from a book the deliberately chosen words of the original writer, and supplying their place by other words which appear to him more suitable?*

In the present case, it is to be observed that Mrs Joceline decidedly

---

* Whoever professes to republish the work of another, is bound surely to give it to the world as the author left it, unless he can show cause for some just exception; in which case, however, he is not entitled furtively to tamper with the text,

approved the use of forms, and certainly did not object to the pre-
scribed forms of prayer used in the Church of England, of which she
was a member. But her heart told her that she had been greatly edi-
fied and comforted by adopting the devotions prepared by a divine
whom she venerated, and who is understood to have been the
admired Puritan, Mr Henry Smith, on whom his biographer, Fuller,
(who himself was not puritanically disposed,) has pronounced the
highest panegyric; while Wood (whose prejudices against scrupulous
divines was still more inveterate) says, 'that this preacher was
esteemed the miracle and wonder of the age, for his prodigious memory, and for his fluent, eloquent, and practical way of preaching.' It is
possible that Mrs Joceline may have meant to recommend the devo-

---

though he may express in a note what he may consider an improvement on the
original. But here is a man in the very peculiar position of announcing the publication of a copy of a lady's last will; and every reader who has no access to the original, and who has not imbibed the doctrine that there is such a thing as 'a pious
fraud,' assuredly takes for granted that, if the editor be even 'indifferent honest,'
the will must be genuine. Nobody for a moment can suspect that any undue liberty had been taken by the Rev. C.H. Craufurd, who, in 1840, appended to a volume of able sermons of his own what he understood to be a reprint of this *Legacy*,
as printed at Oxford in 1684, 'for the satisfaction of the person of quality herein
concerned.' He surely was not capable of corrupting a document written by a pious
female, in the sad and solemn prospect of being severed by death from a beloved
husband and the then unborn infant towards whom her maternal heart was yearn-
ing. Can we conceive it possible that the Oxford licenser, in the days of Bishop
Fell, presumed, without the sanction of a higher authority than his own erring discretion, to vitiate the express words of more than one clause of a writing profess-
edly bearing the character of 'a testament,' as it is described in *The Approbation*,
(p. 3,) by Dr Goad, who expresses his anxiety that its validity may 'be enacted *in
perpetual and inviolable record?'* The violation was not avowed; but the felonious
intent is not palliated by the 'surreptitious practices' through which it was carried
into execution. 'Surreptitious practices,' and 'surreptitious impressions,' are
phrases which occur in the edition of the works of the learned and pious author of
The Whole Duty of Man, printed at Oxford in 1684, (the same year with *The Legacy*,) under the auspices of Bishop Fell; but though he may have improved that edition of an unknown author, it is not alleged that he meddled with Mrs. Joceline's
Legacy. Somebody, however, did meddle; and if there be no intermediate edition
between that of 1625 and the Oxford edition of 1684, we cannot escape from the
conclusion that the tacitly introduced alterations must be traced to Oxford, where
it was alleged that more works than one were altered and interpolated in the time
when Drs Fell and Aldrich were deans of Christ's Church, but by whose hands
cannot now be ascertained. [Lee's reviewer takes him to task for his harsh con-
demnation of the editorial practices of Joscelin's Oxford editor (496).]

tional writings of another divine of the name of Smith – either John Smith, minister at Reading, author of *The Doctrine of Praier in generall for all Men*, printed in 1595, or John Smith, minister and preacher of the Word, who dedicated to Edmund Lord Sheffield, 'A Paterne of True Prayer, being a learned and comfortable Exposition or Commentarie on the Lord's Prayer.' But it scarcely admits of a doubt that her wish was to adopt the prayers interspersed with the sermons of Mr Henry Smith, who (like her grandfather) was specially favoured by the Lord-Treasurer Burghley, who, in proof of his cordial goodwill, concurred with the parishioners of St Clements' Danes in recommending this eloquent preacher to that living ...

It was intended here to insert a list of a number of eminent female writers of high pedigree, and rare attainments in secular learning, who have been distinguished by Christian principle, and by their published compositions, both doctrinal and devotional. It may be enough for the present to refer to Anna Murray, Lady Halket, who was born in the same year with Mrs Joceline's daughter, and who possessed the advantage of a most refined education. Her father, Thomas Murray, (an elegant writer of Latin verse,) of the Earl of Tullibardine's family, was tutor of Charles I., and afterwards Provost of Eton College. Her mother, a daughter of the third Lord Drummond of Perth, was for some time governess to the Princess Elizabeth, afterwards Queen of Bohemia. The father died about two years before his royal pupil's accession to the throne of Great Britain; but the infant family who survived him, (two sons and two daughters,) derived no benefits from the previous connection of their parents with the Court, though all of them continued most steadfastly devoted to the interest of the house of Stuart, and to the principles of the Church of England. Lady Halket appears to have been an indefatigable writer, chiefly on sacred subjects; and her name is here introduced, because, after her marriage to Sir James Halket, (as her biographer, a learned Episcopalian divine, informs us,) 'she wrote what she called *The Mother's WILL to the Unborn Child*, containing excellent instructions.' There is no doubt that a composition with this title was found as the last article in one of more than fifty manuscript volumes found after her death ... It would be very interesting to ascertain if 'The Mother's Will,' as Lady Halket has called it, be an original composition of her own, not suggested by any previous work of a similar character. If she had merely transcribed Mrs Joceline's book, it might have been expected that she would not have varied the title.[1] She was unquestionably qualified in no common degree for writing in a serious and solemn style, of which it would be easy to furnish many pleasing specimens ...

But though much more might be added with regard to the distinguished females who have adorned their Christian profession, it is expedient now to bring this discussion to a close.

I have the honour to be, Madam, your Ladyship's most faithful servant,

THE EDITOR.

College, Edinburgh, Dec. 8, 1851.

Robert Lee (1804–68) was a Presbyterian minister. In 1847, he became the first professor of biblical criticism at the University of Edinburgh. Despite censuring from the Edinburgh presbytery, Lee sought to mitigate the extreme Calvinism prevalent in his church. He introduced reforms to public worship in the Church of Scotland and urged religious tolerance. His liberal views were expressed in numerous devotional works published between 1835 and his death (*DNB* 11: 812–13, Story 1: 205). Although his name does not appear in the 1852 text, Lee is identified as the author of the introduction to *The Mothers Legacie* in *The National Union Catalogue* (281: 164).

---

1 Lee refers to a biography of Anne Halkett (1622–99) published in 1701; the author is identified only as S.C. 'The Mother's Will to her Unborn Child,' written during Halkett's first pregnancy, is considered to be lost (Blain, Grundy, and Clements, 475). Sophia Blaydes records that Halkett wrote a similar tract during each of her three later pregnancies (213).

2 SARAH JOSEPHA HALE (1871)

The / Mothers Legacie, / To Her / Vnborne Childe. / By / Elizabeth Ioceline. / From the Edition of 1625. / Edited, with an Introduction, / By Mrs. S.J. Hale. / Philadelphia: / Duffield Ashmead. / 1871.

Dedication.

To the Reader who honors the feminine character,
this little Book is offered as a touching
example of a woman's self-sacri-
ficing love. May these
utterances from
the pure soul of a tender
wife and mother, speaking across
the chasm of more than two centuries, teach
lessons of true wisdom to the daughters of America.

SARAH JOSEPHA HALE.

Introduction.

THE little book here republished was sent to the Editress by a friend, upon whom its simplicity and pathos had made a deep impression. In the accompanying letter he says, 'To my mind, The Mother's Legacie is simply the most touching thing which has been written; I think no one can read her letter to her husband without tears.' This is, for any book, an extreme measure of praise; and the Editress, concurring with it, has brought The Mother's Legacie before the American public. The English reprint of 1853 [*sic*], from which this edition is made, is encumbered by a tedious and partly irrelevant introduction, in lieu of which the Editress offers these few pages, to explain the circumstances under which the book was written, and her reasons for the republication.

The Mother's Legacie was written some two hundred and fifty years ago by Elizabeth Joceline, who had then been married six years. Her maiden name was Brooke. While she was yet a child, her mother died; and Elizabeth's early years were passed under the roof of her grandfather, Bishop Chaderton, a man of equal learning and piety. There she was trained both to mental and moral excellence. That age showed, by many examples, the capacity of women for a sound and thorough education, and in all the learning of the schools, especially in the Greek and Latin, which then represented learning to Christendom, she was no unworthy compeer of Lady Jane Grey and Lady Cecil. To the careful training of her grandfather, we may also ascribe that vital piety which was the foundation of her character, and has impressed itself upon every line of this memorial to her child. In 1616 she married Mr. Tourell Joceline. We know him only through his wife; but her love for him and her faith in him were so great, that we may well see him with her eyes.

After a happy married life of six years, her time being near, she wrote this Letter, that if she died in childbirth, her baby might not wholly lose the influence of her teaching. With the Legacie she left a letter to her husband, so loving and tender, so full of womanly sweetness and humility, that the book may serve for mothers as well as children; leaving to him the charge of her unborn child, and the performance of her wishes.

The event against whose consequences she had striven to guard unhappily came to pass. After the birth of her child, she fell sick of a fever, which in nine days ended her life. She died in October, 1622, in her twenty-seventh year.

The Legacie was printed in 1625, having received Bishop Goad's approbation. It has been reprinted at least three times: in 1684, in 1840, and again in 1853 by Blackwood and Sons. In that edition, as in this, the original spelling has been carefully preserved. It differs from that of the present day in so few particulars, that no difficulty will be felt by the reader; while the verisimilitude of the work is preserved. 'The morality of the book,' says our friend, 'is far above the standard of the age, and shows the dawn of the Puritanical spirit. I see nothing in it which we would not now accept as the true teaching of the Gospel.' With the ideas we have preserved as well the form of the age. Yet it is singular how perfect is the application of the book to the wants of our domestic life. It speaks of things that can never grow old, that will endure so long as the household endures. The affection of a wife, the solicitude of a mother, speak to us over the gulf of centuries with an accent as distinct and as touching as the voice of yesterday. It is for this reason that the Editress has ventured, in a time when children's books may be counted by hundreds, to offer the Legacie to American Protestants. The vitality of the little book, the hold which it takes on its readers, has been sufficiently shown. Ever and anon, a new edition has kept alive the writer's memory in her native land. The Editress hopes that, in America as well, its beauty and its wisdom will commend it to Christian hearts.

PHILADELPHIA: October, 1870.

Sarah Josepha (Buell) Hale was born in New Hampshire in 1788. She published some minor poetry during her marriage, but, following her husband's premature death, she became a prolific author and prominent editor of women's magazines. By the time of her death in 1879, she had written or edited fifty books. Although Hale was opposed to the women's sufferage movement, she actively promoted the improvement of women's education and she championed women as spiritually superior to men (James, James, and Boyer 2: 110–14).

3 RANDALL T. DAVIDSON (1894)

The / Mother's Legacy / To Her Unborn Child / By Elizabeth Joceline / Anno 1622 / Reprinted from the 6th Impression / with an Introduction by the / Lord Bishop of Rochester / London: Macmillan and Co. / And New York / 1894

Introduction

GO to the British Museum. Turn into the Manuscript Department, and ask for MS. No. 27,467. A tiny volume will be handed to you, containing, within a modern cover of blue velvet, some eighty-six little pages of close and careful writing, and a good many others which are blank. The writing is clear and small, but it is not strictly uniform, and both the ink and the penmanship show that, though every word is written by the same hand, the task was often interrupted and resumed. The alterations and corrections in the manuscript – though not very numerous after all – make it certain that we have before us the original and not a copy.

Towards the end the writing becomes less regular and careful, and the last few pages in particular, vigorous and legible as they are, bear unmistakable signs of physical difficulty or distress.

Such is *The Mother's Legacie* in its original form, the handiwork of Elizabeth Jocelin, a few weeks or days before she died, on October 12, 1622. If ever book or letter upon earth told its own story, it is this; and it would be inexcusable to mar its simple pathos by a single line of paraphrase or explanation. A few details of a biographical sort may however have an interest, and may even throw light upon some pages of the *Legacie*.

In 1608 died William Chaderton, who had been successively Fellow of Christ's College, Cambridge, chaplain to Robert Dudley, Earl of Leicester, Professor of Divinity, Master of Queen's College, Bishop of Chester, and Bishop of Lincoln. A refined scholar, a keen controversialist, and a stern opponent of 'Popish recusants,' he was a close friend of Bishop Lancelot Andrewes and of other men like minded. In 1569 he married Katherine Revell, by whom he had one child, Joan, born in 1574. In her nineteenth year Joan married a Cheshire squire, Sir Richard Brooke of Norton. The marriage was not a happy one, and Lady Brooke was separated from her husband soon after the birth in

1595 of their only daughter, Elizabeth. When Elizabeth was six years old her mother died, and the child was committed to the care of her grandfather, Bishop Chaderton, then resident at Lincoln. Under his loving guardianship, as we are told, 'shee was from her tender yeeres carefully nurtured, as in those accomplishments of knowledge in Languages, History, and some Arts, so principally in studies of piety.'

In 1616 she married Tourell Jocelin, a gentleman of Cambridge-shire, about whom nothing seems to be known but what may be gathered from the letter of his wife. The sequel is told in the 'Appro-bation' of Dr. Thomas Goad, prefixed to the *Legacie* when it was first published in 1624, and here reprinted in its place. Dr. Goad, who is described by Fuller, in his *Worthies of England*, as having 'a com-manding presence, an uncontrolable spirit, impatient to be opposed, and loving to steer the discourse of all the company he came in,' was Rector of Hadleigh, and domestic chaplain to Abbot, Archbishop of Canterbury. It was doubtless in this capacity, and on the Arch-bishop's behalf, that he prefixed the 'Approbation' to this little book.

The *Legacie*, though written 'onely to the eyes of a most louing Husband, and of a childe exceedingly beloued,' was published two years later, in 1624. A second edition appeared in the same year, a third in 1625, and three others in the course of the next seven years. It has since been republished in 1684, in 1724, in 1840, in 1852, and in 1853. In the editions of 1684, 1724, and 1840 the text was in places deliberately altered, without explanation or excuse, to suit the taste, it would seem, of 'a person of quality herein concerned.' A Dutch translation was published in Amsterdam in 1678 and was reprinted in 1748. The present edition is an exact reprint of the impression of 1632.

No apology can be required for placing it again in the hands of all who can appreciate, along with the simple pathos of its history, the rare combination it presents of earnest piety, quiet womanly counsel, and vigorous common sense.

RANDALL T. ROFFEN:

All Saints' Day, 1893.

Randall Thomas Davidson (1848–1930) was the Bishop of Rochester from 1891–5. Thus, he signs his introduction to *The Mother's Legacy* 'Roffen,' the Latin form of Rochester. Davidson, a confidante to Queen Victoria, went on to become Archbishop of Canterbury (1903–28). His biographer, G.K.A. Bell, does not mention Davidson's contribution to the edition.

Index

The page numbers for *The Mothers Legacy to her Vnborn Childe* refer to Joscelin's manuscript; the corresponding reference in the 1624 edition will be found on the right-hand page. The page numbers of illustrations appear in italics.